How to Start a Conversation and Make Friends

Revised and Updated

Don Gabor

Illustrated by Mary Power

A TOUCHSTONE BOOK
Published by Simon & Schuster
New York   London   Toronto   Sydney

Touchstone
A Division of Simon & Schuster, Inc.
1230 Avenue of the Americas
New York, NY 10020

First Touchstone trade paperback edition June 2011

TOUCHSTONE and colophon are registered trademarks of Simon & Schuster, Inc.

For information about special discounts for bulk purchases, please contact Simon & Schuster Special Sales at 1-866-506-1949 or business@simonandschuster.com.

The Simon & Schuster Speakers Bureau can bring authors to your live event. For more information or to book an event, contact the Simon & Schuster Speakers Bureau at 866-248-3049 or visit our website at www.simonspeakers.com.

Manufactured in the United States of America

20 19 18 17

Library of Congress Cataloging-in-Publication Data

Gabor, Don.
    How to start a conversation and make friends / by Don Gabor ; illustrated by
    Mary Power.—[Rev. ed.].
        p. cm.
    "A Touchstone book."
    Includes index.
    1. Conversation. 2. Friendship. I. Power, Mary. II. Title.
    BJ2121.G3 2011
    153.6—dc22

                                                                2011008739

ISBN 978-1-4516-1099-4
ISBN 978-0-7432-1291-5 (ebook)

I dedicate this book to my parents, Trude and Fred, and my sister, Ellen.

Thank you for giving me the confidence and encouragement to talk to anyone, anyplace, about anything.

I also dedicate this book to my wife and the love of my life, Eileen.

Contents

Acknowledgments

My special thanks go to:

My wife, Eileen Cowell, for her loving and continued support, many excellent editorial suggestions, and more than twenty-five years of rewarding and insightful conversations.

My editors, Michelle Howry and Alessandra Preziosi, at Simon & Schuster for their enthusiasm, many useful ideas, and belief in this project.

My agent, Herb Schaffner, for helping me bring this project to Simon & Schuster and all his efforts on my behalf.

Jeffrey Hollender for the original opportunity to develop my conversation course in 1980 and the first edition of this book in 1983.

A Note from the Author

How to Start a Conversation and Make Friends was first published in 1983 and revised in 2001. Since then, I have written several books and presented many workshops on conversation skills to people all over the country. Still, even after all my years of teaching, writing, and talking about this subject, I realize there is always something to learn about the art of conversation.

The revisions in this book are based on feedback and questions from hundreds of readers and students, plus additional research and personal experience. I have reorganized the book into four parts: "Starting Your Conversations with Confidence"; "Continuing and Ending Your Conversations with Charm, Confidence, and Tact"; "Navigating Online Networks to Expand Your Business, Social, and Personal Relationships"; and "Boosting Your Conversations to the Next Level."

Included in these sections are new and revised chapters on body language; knowing what to say after you say hello; telling others about yourself; remembering names; dealing with awkward conversations; exploring social networks; making contacts and friends online; networking; starting and rekindling friendships; dating; conversation styles; talking to people from other countries; plus a final list of 60 ways to improve your conversations and build lasting friendships. There are also many frequently asked questions (FAQs) throughout the text.

Most people want and need human contact, and that connection often takes the form of a simple conversation. The secret to starting conversations and making friends rests on four key principles: (1) taking the initiative to reach out to others; (2) showing genuine interest in people; (3) treating others with respect and kindness; and (4) valuing others and yourself as unique individuals who have much to share and offer one another. When you apply these ideas and the many other skills and tips in this book, you can become a great conversationalist. I hope that this newly revised edition will help you achieve this goal.

Introduction:
Meeting New People and Making
New Friends—It's What Today's Success
Is All About!

> Good conversation is what makes us interesting. After all, we
> spend a great deal of our time talking and a great deal of our
> time listening. Why be bored, why be boring—when you don't
> have to be either?
> —Edwin Newman (1919–2010), news commentator

The next time you walk into a room full of people, just listen to
them talking! They're all communicating through conversation.
Conversation is our main way of expressing our ideas, opinions,
goals, and feelings to those we come into contact with. It is also
the primary means of beginning and establishing friendships and
relationships.

Open Your Conversation Channel in Person and Online via Social Networks

Whether we meet people at parties, at work, or on social networking sites like Facebook or LinkedIn, we can connect and communicate with those people when the "channel of conversation"
is open. If the channel is closed, then starting and sustaining a
conversation and creating a relationship of any kind is next to
impossible.

This book is based on my more than thirty years teaching and
writing about how to start a conversation and make friends. It will
show you how to open your conversational channel and tune in
to the people you meet in your daily activities and online through

social networks. The conversational techniques in this book have been successfully tested in my workshops and proven as methods of starting and sustaining conversations in nearly every situation—including social and business settings.

The techniques are presented in an easy-to-master format so you can start improving your communication skills and self-confidence quickly. Hundreds of examples demonstrate what you can say in real-life situations so you can practice and adapt them within the context of your own lifestyle and at your own pace.

This book can be helpful to anyone who wants to communicate better at home, at work, online, or anywhere in between, including:

- Business executives, managers, and new hires
- Members of Facebook, LinkedIn, and other social networks
- Consultants and sales representatives
- Singles and couples
- Computer programmers and other technical professionals
- Entrepreneurs and freelancers
- English language learners
- Career counselors and life coaches
- Psychologists, therapists, and clients
- Students and teachers
- Parents and teenagers

If you want more rewarding conversations in professional, social, or personal situations, then this book is for you.

How This Book Can Help You

Many people who attend my workshops, read my books, and listen to my audio programs are making career changes, and they want to learn how to move easily into new social and work environments. Singles want to get to know people first online before they meet in person for a date. Salespeople want to know how to converse and build rapport with clients in an informal manner. Executives and managers want to increase their staffs' productivity and loyalty. Entrepreneurs and freelancers want to make their networking pay off. New residents of the United States want to learn conversational English. Couples want to communicate better with each other and their families. You can achieve all of these communication goals and more by improving your conversation skills.

Even good conversationalists sometimes find themselves in awkward situations where the conversation is just not going the way they want it to. This book provides techniques and the exact words you can use to help you better direct and control the conversation at such times.

Learn to Enjoy Parties while Winning New Friends

Perhaps the most common situation that causes problems for many is meeting new people and socializing at parties and social events. Surveys show that many people feel uncomfortable in a room full of strangers and are anxious about approaching others. This book presents practical skills for meeting new people, making new friends, and developing lasting and meaningful relationships.

Most people want to share their experiences with others. We are constantly searching for others we can relate to on an intellectual, physical, and emotional level. This search can be frustrating and unfulfilling if you aren't able to reach out and connect. Once you master the basic fundamentals of good conversation and are willing to reach out, you'll be open and available for new friendships and relationships.

You Can Learn to Communicate and Use New Skills

The ability to communicate in an informal and friendly manner is essential for every aspect of a person's business, social, and personal life. Most people can converse with others when they feel confident and comfortable. The problem arises when comfort and confidence are replaced by anxiety and fear. This book will help you identify which communication skills have worked for you and in which situations you feel confident.

Once you understand the skills that promote natural conversations, then begin using them in situations where you feel comfortable and confident. You will be able to see how effective you are while simultaneously integrating these new techniques into your lifestyle.

As you become more confident with your conversational skills in "safe" situations, take some extra risks and begin to use your new communication skills in situations where you were previously uncomfortable and anxious. You'll be pleasantly surprised to find that your skills will transfer from one situation to another far more easily than you ever imagined. As your control increases, so will your confidence. Your ability to maintain casual and sustained conversations will become part of your personality. Don't think about the skills and techniques too much; just let them become a natural basis for communicating.

Connect with People in Traditional and Modern Ways

The goal of this conversation book is to help you meet people in traditional ways where you work, live, worship, and play. It will also help you connect in what has become a modern and popular way to socialize: online through social networks, blogs, and dating websites. Whether face-to-face or online, we have much to gain by communicating in an open and mutual manner. By sharing our experiences, we can grow in new ways. Our horizons and opportunities can expand, while our relationships may deepen and become more meaningful. Friendships and a sense of personal fulfillment can develop.

Getting Started: Pick Any Chapter to Begin

You don't have to read the entire book from cover to cover to get started. Take a look at the table of contents, see what topics appeal to you the most, and turn to those chapters. By putting conversation tips, skills, and techniques into practice right away, you'll see how quickly you can integrate them into your daily activities and improve your ability to communicate and connect with those around you.

Make it your goal to reach out to others and create new relationships by using the ideas presented in this book. See how the tips, techniques, skills, and examples work for you. Then tweak and adapt them to get even better results. When you take this approach, I promise that you will find that breaking the ice, meeting people, and making new friends is easier and more fun than you thought! So, let's begin and . . . start a conversation!

Part I

Starting Your Conversations
with Confidence

Closed body language sends out the message "Stay away! I'd rather be left alone!"

First Contact: Body Language

"It's a luxury to be understood."
—Ralph Waldo Emerson (1803–1882),
American poet and essayist

One of our most important conversational skills doesn't come from our tongue, but from our body. Research has shown that over half of face-to-face conversation is nonverbal. "Body language," as it is called, often communicates our feelings and attitudes before we speak, and it projects our level of receptivity to others.

Most poor conversationalists don't realize that their nonreceptive body language (crossed arms, little eye contact, and no smiling) is often the cause of short and unsustained conversations. We are judged quickly by the first signals we give off, and if the first impressions are not open and friendly, it's going to be difficult to maintain a good conversation.

The following "softening" techniques can make your first impressions work for you, not against you.

S-O-F-T-E-N

In his excellent book on shyness, *Making Contact*, Arthur C. Wassmer coined the term *SOFTEN* as a way to remember six body language "softeners." A softener is a nonverbal gesture that will make people more responsive and receptive to you. Since your body language speaks before you do, it is important to project a receptive image. When you use open body language, you are already sending the signal: "I'm friendly and willing to communicate, if you are." Each letter in S-O-F-T-E-N represents a specific nonverbal technique for encouraging others to talk with you.

"S-O-F-T-E-N" Your Body Language

- **S = Smile**
- **O = Open Arms**
- **F = Forward Lean**
- **T = Touch**
- **E = Eye Contact**
- **N = Nod**

Use your body language to break down the natural barriers that separate strangers.

S = Smile

A pleasant *smile* is a strong indication of a friendly and open attitude and a willingness to communicate. It is a receptive, nonverbal signal sent with the hope that the other person will smile back.

When you smile, you demonstrate that you have noticed the person in a positive manner. The other person considers it a compliment and will usually feel good. The result? The other person will usually smile back.

Smiling does not mean that you have to put on a phony face or pretend that you are happy all of the time. But when you see someone you know or would like to make contact with, do smile. By smiling, you are demonstrating an open attitude to conversation.

A smile shows you are friendly and open to communication. When you frown or wrinkle your brow, you give off signals of skepticism and nonreceptivity.

The human face sends out an enormous number of verbal and nonverbal signals. If you send out friendly messages, you're going to get friendly messages back. When you couple a warm smile with a friendly hello, you'll be pleasantly surprised by similar responses. It's the easiest and best way to show someone that you've noticed him. A smile indicates general approval toward the other person, and this will usually make the other person feel more open to talk to you.

O = Open Arms

The letter *O* in S-O-F-T-E-N stands for *open arms*. You've probably been welcomed "with open arms," which, of course, means that a person was glad to see you. At a party or in another social or business situation, open arms suggest that you are friendly and available for contact. During a conversation, open arms make others feel that you are receptive and listening.

Crossed arms say: "I'm thinking and don't want to be disturbed. Stay away!"

Open arms say: "I'm receptive and available for contact."

On the other hand, standing or sitting with your arms crossed makes you appear closed to contact, defensive, and closed-minded. Add a hand covering your mouth (and your smile) or your chin and you are practically in the classic "thinking" pose. Now, just ask yourself this question: Are you going to interrupt someone who appears to be deep in thought? Probably not. In addition, crossing your arms tends to make you appear nervous, judgmental, or skeptical—all of which discourage people from approaching you or feeling comfortable while talking to you.

Some people argue that just because they have their arms crossed, it doesn't mean that they are closed to conversation. They say, "I cross my arms because I'm comfortable that way." The arm crossers may be comfortable, but the problem is that while no one can read minds, most people can read body language. Crossed arms say: "Stay away" and "My mind is made up." Open arms say: "I'm available for contact and willing to listen. Come on over and talk to me."

F = Forward Lean

The letter *F* in S-O-F-T-E-N means *forward lean*. Leaning forward slightly while a person is talking to you indicates interest on your part and shows you are listening to what the person is saying. This is usually taken as a compliment by the other person, and will encourage him to continue talking.

Leaning back gives off signals of disinterest and even boredom.

Leaning forward says: "I'm interested in what you're saying."

Often people will lean back with their hands over their mouths or chins, or behind their heads in the "relaxing" pose. Unfortunately, this posture gives off signals that the listener is judging you, skeptical, or bored. Since most people do not feel comfortable when they think they are being judged, this leaning-back posture tends to inhibit the speaker from continuing.

When you are in a conversation, it's far better to lean forward slightly in a casual and natural way. By doing this, you are saying: "I hear what you're saying, and I'm interested: Keep talking!" This usually helps the other person feel confident and encourages him to continue speaking.

Defining Personal Space

Personal space, or standing distance, is an important part of body language. However, what's comfortable varies widely depending on a person's culture, social situation, gender, and preference. Tuning in to, understanding, and respecting the personal space of others help eliminate discomfort that people may feel when they stand too close or too far away from each other as they speak. Personal space boundaries for many North Americans depend on the type of conversation.

- **Intimate distance:** 0 to 18 inches (0 to 0.4 meter) for conversations between spouses, family, and people who are embracing, touching, or whispering.

- **Personal distance:** 18 to 36 inches (0.4 to 0.9 meter) for conversations between good friends, family, or informal acquaintances—people who want to get to know one another better and in a more personal way.

- **Social distance:** 3 to 5 feet (0.9 to 1.5 meters) for more formal conversations between business or formal social acquaintances.

For more specific standing distances in different cultures, see "How Savvy Are You about the Customs of Other Cultures?" in chapter 18.

T = Touch

The letter *T* in *S-O-F-T-E-N* stands for *touch*. In Western culture, the most acceptable form of first contact between two people who are just meeting is a warm handshake. This is usually true when meeting members of the same or opposite sex in business and in social situations too. In nearly every situation, a warm and firm handshake is a safe way of showing an open and friendly attitude toward the people you meet.

Be the first to extend your hand in greeting. Couple this hand-shake with a friendly "Hi!" and a nice smile and your name, and you have made the first step to open the channels of communication between you and the other person.

Some men don't feel right in offering their hand to a woman first. They say they would feel stupid if the woman didn't shake their hand. Emily Post states in the revised edition of her book of etiquette that it is perfectly acceptable for a man to offer a hand-shake to a woman and that, in most cases, it would be rude for either man or woman to ignore or refuse this friendly gesture.

However, because of cultural and age differences, some women might feel that they are being too forward if they offer a hand-shake to a man. They think the man might "get the wrong idea" if they extend their hand first in greeting. The problem then is that there are two people who are afraid to shake hands. Although there are some exceptions because of religious customs, most of the people I've polled on the subject agree: no matter who makes the first move, nearly everyone likes this form of physical contact. A handshake is safe and nonthreatening for both parties. This keeps personal defenses down and creates an atmosphere of equality and receptivity between the people. More personal forms of touch should be exercised with a sensitivity to the other person's culture and in a warm, nonaggressive manner.

It is also important to end your conversations with a warm and friendly handshake in business and social situations. Combine it with a bright smile and a friendly statement like "I've really enjoyed talking with you!" or "Let's get together again soon." This is an excellent way to end a conversation and leaves you and the other person both feeling good about the exchange.

A friendly handshake with a smile and a warm "Hello. . . . Nice to meet you!" is an easy, acceptable form of touch when meeting someone for the first time.

E = Eye Contact

The letter *E* in *S-O-F-T-E-N* represents *eye contact*. Perhaps the strongest nonverbal gestures are made with the eyes. Direct eye contact indicates that you are listening to the other person and that you want to know more about him or her. With eye contact and a friendly smile, you'll send this unmistakable message: "I'd like to talk to you and maybe get to know you better."

Eye contact should be natural and not forced or overdone. It is perfectly okay to have brief periods of eye contact while you observe other parts of the person's face, particularly the mouth. When the person smiles, be sure to smile back. But always make an effort to return your gaze to the person's eyes as she speaks. It is common to look up, down, and all around when speaking to others, and it's acceptable not to have eye contact every second.

Too much eye contact can be counterproductive. If you stare at a person, she may feel uncomfortable and even suspicious about your intentions. A fixed stare can be interpreted as aggressive behavior if it takes the form of a challenge as to who will look away first. It is not wise to employ eye contact as a "power struggle," because it will usually result in a negative, defensive response from the other person.

Also, be aware that eye contact varies widely from culture to culture. For example, North Americans and Europeans typically have medium to strong eye contact. However, in Mexico, you will be viewed with suspicion if you have eye contact for too long. In many Asian cultures, averting the eyes is a mark of respect. Some Middle Eastern and Asian cultures and religions have strict rules against women making any direct eye contact with men. (For more about the cultural differences regarding eye contact, see "How Savvy Are You About the Customs of Other Cultures?" in chapter 18.)

FAQ

I feel uncomfortable making direct eye contact. What can I do?

If you have a problem maintaining comfortable eye contact, try these suggestions. Start with short periods of eye contact—maybe only a few seconds. Look into the pupils of the other person's eyes, and smile. Then let your gaze travel over the features of his face, hair, nose, lips, and even earlobes! There is a three-inch radius around the eyes that can provide a visual pathway. After a few moments, go back to looking the person directly in the eyes. As the conversation continues, you can look back and forth between both eyes while increasing the amount of time that you make direct eye contact.

Avoiding eye contact can make both parties feel anxious and uncomfortable and can give the impression that you are uninterested, dishonest, or bored with the conversation and the company. The result will usually be a short and unfulfilling conversation. So be sure to look into the eyes of the people you talk with and send this message: "I'm paying attention and want to hear more."

Eye contact shows that you are listening and taking an interest in what is being said. It sends the signal "I'm listening—keep talking."

N = Nod

The letter *N* in *S-O-F-T-E-N* stands for *nod*. A nod of the head indicates that you are listening and that you understand what is being said. It usually signals approval and encourages the other person to continue talking. A nod of the head, along with a smile and a friendly hello, is an excellent way of greeting people on the street or anywhere else. Like all the other softening gestures, it sends the same message: "I'm friendly and willing to communicate."

A nod of the head shows you are listening and understand what is being said. A blank stare suggests your thoughts are elsewhere.

However, in a conversation, a nod does not necessarily mean agreement. If you want to be sure someone agrees with what you're saying, ask, "Do you agree?"

Body Language and Mirroring

Most people don't realize it, but they frequently *mirror* or subtly mimic body movements and expressions of the people they talk to. Many studies have shown that mirroring increases rapport and facilitates conversation. For example, when someone with whom you are chatting smiles at you, you smile back. If she leans forward slightly in her chair to show interest, you do the same. In most cases, mirroring positive body language makes both speakers more open and talkative. However, mirroring negative or closed body language—folded arms, little eye contact, or not shaking hands—tends to decrease levels of comfort, rapport, and trust.

FAQ

What do mixed body language signals mean?

It's common in a conversation for people to send a mixture of receptive and nonreceptive body language messages. For example, sometimes in a conversation they smile but at the same time cross their arms or have little eye contact. The smile says, "I'm interested," but the folded arms and poor eye contact suggest skepticism or a lack of interest. Therefore, instead of assuming you understand the other person's perspective when he or she sends you mixed or negative body language signals, ask a few clarification questions. This will give the other person an opportunity to clarify or elaborate on his or her views or feelings. For example, you can say, "Tell me a little more about . . . ?" or "What do you mean when you say . . . ?"

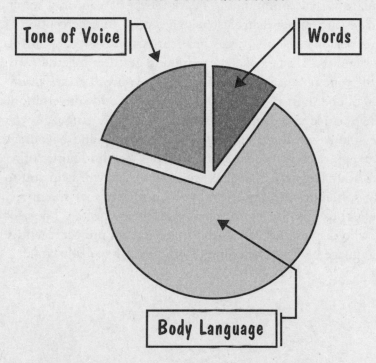

Your body language speaks *before* you do. Research has shown that over two-thirds of face-to-face conversation is based on body language. Along with the tone of your voice and the words you use, they add up to "total communication."

Body Language + Tone of Voice + Words = Total Communication

Keep in mind that effective communication is a combination of body language, tone of voice, and words. When you look for and use a combination of these softening gestures together with a friendly tone of voice and inviting words, you will create an impression of openness and availability for contact and conversation. Remember that these nonverbal softening gestures alone do not replace verbal communication. Moreover, if you only see an isolated gesture, rather than clusters of gestures, your perception of the other person's receptivity may be incorrect. However, when you look for and use clusters of these softening gestures together with a friendly tone of voice and inviting words, you will create an impression of openness and availability for contact and conversation.

With practice and a greater awareness of body language, you will be able to send and receive receptive signals and encourage others to approach you and feel comfortable. Begin to notice other people's body language as well as your own. This will help you to identify softening techniques and recognize levels of receptivity in others, thus minimizing the chance of being rejected. Look for people who display receptive body language, and project receptive body language by using softening techniques. They really work!

2

Four Natural Ways to
Break the Ice

Ideal conversation must be an exchange of thought, and not,
as many of those who worry most about their shortcomings
believe, an eloquent exhibition of wit or oratory.
—Emily Post (1872–1960), writer and authority on etiquette

Take a Risk and Be the First to Say Hello

It takes a certain amount of risk to begin a conversation with a
stranger. Many people don't start conversations because they fear
being rejected. Of course, this prevents them from reaching out
to others. Remember that risk taking and rejection are part of
life, and being overly sensitive about how others react to you is
counterproductive. Anyway, what's so bad about being rejected by
someone you don't even know?

Take an Active Role

Most shy people take the passive role when it comes to starting
conversations. They wait and wait and wait, hoping someone will
come along and start a conversation with them. If there are two
shy people together, they're both waiting, both taking the passive
role. If someone else by chance does start talking, the shy person is
often so surprised, he or she doesn't know what to say.

To get out of this catch-22, consciously change from the passive
to the active role. Be the first to say hello and take the initiative by
beginning the conversation. Introduce yourself to people regularly
and begin to share your ideas, feelings, opinions, and experiences.

Look for familiar faces and, after saying hello, seek out other people's thoughts, views, and interests. By initiating conversations, you'll get more positive responses and your fear of rejection will lessen. In this way your risk taking can pay off in making new contacts and having more meaningful conversations.

Another advantage of being the first to say hello is that it gives you the opportunity to guide the direction of the conversation, and gives the other person the impression that you are confident, friendly, and open. You are also complimenting the other person by showing a desire to start a conversation with him or her.

Four Ways to Start Conversations

Ask a closed-ended or open-ended question

Make a positive or lighthearted comment

Offer a compliment followed by an easy-to-answer question

Introduce yourself

Changing topics is easy if you say, "I heard you mention earlier . . ." or "Speaking of . . . ," then ask a question or share information about a general or specific topic related to key words you hear.

If You See Something, Say Something

Icebreaker #1: Ask Closed- and Open-ended Ritual Questions

The easiest way to start a conversation with a stranger is to ask an easy-to-answer "ritual" question. Ritual questions are commonly asked short-answer questions about where a person works and lives. Ritual questions often refer to a person's occupation, background, education, family, and upbringing; for example: "What kind of work do you do?" "Where do you live?" "What did you study in school?" "Where did you grow up?"

Most people are open to answering ritual questions as long as you do not ask too many in a row and that the questions are not overly personal. Because ritual questions are familiar requests for background information, they require little time and thought to answer. These kinds of questions are good for breaking the ice and starting a conversation. By looking for what people are involved in, you can easily focus on a topic of interest to the other person. Remember, in addition to finding out about the other person, you are sending this signal: "You seem interesting to me, and I'd like to talk to you."

Closed-ended Ritual Questions Require Only a Short Answer

Closed-ended ritual questions usually call for only a yes or a no, or just a one- or two-word answer. They are "fishing" questions because you're looking for a "bite" on a particular topic. If you get a positive response, you can usually follow up with another question or a comment that will open up the conversation. Closed-ended questions often begin with: "Are . . . ?" "Do . . . ?" "Who . . . ?" "Where . . . ?" "When . . . ?" "What . . . ?" "How . . . ?" or "Which . . . ?"

Here are some common examples of closed-ended ritual questions you can ask where you live, work, and play:

Do you live around here?
What's your favorite team?
What's your (dog's) name?
Where are you from?
Who else was at the party?
Are you enjoying your stay?
Which do you recommend?
Is this your first visit here?
Which do you prefer?
Who do you know at . . . that I might know?

Closed-ended questions are useful for breaking the ice and finding out some basic facts, but they are more effective when followed with an open-ended question.

Ask Closed- & Open-ended Questions

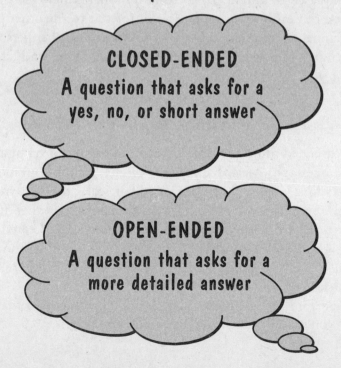

CLOSED-ENDED
A question that asks for a
yes, no, or short answer

OPEN-ENDED
A question that asks for a
more detailed answer

Open-ended Questions Require a More Detailed Response

Open-ended questions encourage the other person to talk. In addition, they provide an opportunity to reveal facts, opinions, feelings, and, most important, plenty of additional information. They often start with "What made you decide . . . ?" "In what way?" "How so?" "How did you . . . ?" "Can you tell me more about . . . ?" or "Why?"

Here are some examples of open-ended questions you can ask where you live, work, and play:

> *Can you tell me why you feel that way?*
> *In what ways do you think . . . has changed?*
> *How did you get involved in that line of work?*
> *Why did you decide to move there?*
> *What brings you to our town?*
> *What do you like to do on your days off?*
> *What is it about . . . that you like so much?*
> *How would you handle that situation?*

More about Ritual Questions

Ritual questions allow you to reveal basic personal information in a natural and informal way. By exchanging little details with another person, you can get to know something about him or her. Ritual questions help you to find out and disclose background information and provide an opportunity to discover the "big" things in a person's life. They also help you quickly determine if you would like to get to know this person better.

Ask ritual questions when you want to break the ice or change topics in conversation. If your ritual question gets a brief reply, try another until you get an enthusiastic response. When you discover an area of interest in the other person, be sure to follow with open-ended information-seeking questions, but don't do it "machine gun" style. When the topic seems to be running out of steam (you don't have to talk a subject completely out), return to another ritual question based on free information that you or the other person revealed earlier.

If you employ these ritual question techniques for breaking the ice with the people you meet, you'll discover they really do work. Being the first to say hello won't be a problem any longer. I base my ritual question on my surroundings and:

- What the person is doing, wearing, or saying
- Something that I need or I'm looking for
- Something I think the person may need or is looking for
- Something that I'm curious about that I think that he or she might be able to answer

Using closed- and open-ended ritual questions can certainly get a conversation going. When I'm starting a conversation, I like to fish for topics of interest with one or two closed questions. If I get a positive response, I'll encourage the person to elaborate by asking a few open-ended questions. I make my questions easy and straightforward. That's because most people are far more comfortable answering expected, easy-to-answer questions when they first meet a person, rather than difficult or complicated questions that put them on the spot.

Note: If you're only getting one- or two-word answers from someone, it's probably because you are asking too many closed-ended questions. Try sprinkling in some open-ended questions and watch your conversation open up.

FAQ

How do I break the ice at a networking event or party with two or three people who are already talking to each other?

To enter a conversation in progress, you must be within listening and speaking range. Move close to the people speaking and show interest in what is being said. Use plenty of eye contact, nodding, and smiling to send the signal to the speakers that you want to hear more. Often, when a speaker sees you are interested in what he is saying, he will begin to include you as a listener.

When there is a pause or the speaker says something you can respond to, then interject your comment or question into the conversation. If you use easy-to-answer information questions, the answers will be directed to you specifically. Say something like "What did you do next?" or "How did that happen?" or "That's a truly incredible story! How long ago did this happen?"

To join a conversation in progress, follow these steps:

Step 1: Look for small open groups of friendly-looking people.

Step 2: Move within communicating distance (about three feet).

Step 3: Establish eye contact and smile at the speakers.

Step 4: Ask a question, make a positive comment, or give a compliment followed by a question.

Step 5: Introduce yourself and say, "Do you mind if I join you?"

You may be saying to yourself that this is an intrusion into a private conversation. If you have listened and carefully observed the people, you will quickly be able to determine if they are receptive. In many cases, especially at networking functions, most attendees are searching for others to interact with, and a new person who shows interest in participating is usually welcome.

Caution: Be careful not to play devil's advocate—that is, to take an opposing position for the sake of argument. This usually leads to a tense and competitive conversation, with a winner and a loser. You won't be considered a welcome addition to a conversation with a group of strangers if you make them look stupid or embarrass them in front of their friends or colleagues.

You Can Break the Ice Anywhere You Want

Whenever I'm standing in front of a restaurant, I'll ask a customer going in or out, "Is this a good place to eat?" or "Do you know their specialty?" or "Can you recommend an appetizer or entrée?" If I'm at a party, I'll ask another guest, "What do you think of the dip?" In the grocery store, I'll ask another shopper, "Would you happen to know which of the . . . I can use for . . . ?" or "I'm looking for some inspiration. What are you cooking for dinner tonight?" or "That looks interesting. How do you prepare that?" or "Would you happen to know what kind of . . . this is?"

Show Curiosity and Interest in Others

If you see someone using a fancy laptop, you can ask her if she likes it, where she got it, and the features she likes best. If you see someone reading a travel book, you could ask him if he's planning a trip and what some interesting things to do there are. These kinds of questions can be applied to almost any situation and are a safe and friendly way of showing others that you are interested in engaging in conversation.

Seeking Information Is an Easy Way to Break the Ice

"Excuse me, may I ask you a question?" is a natural way to break the ice with a stranger. If I get a smile and nod, I continue, "I'm looking for a . . . in the neighborhood. Do you happen to know of any . . . ?" Another way to break the ice is to ask if someone needs assistance. In your neighborhood or building, you can say, "Are you looking for someone? Maybe I can help you." In the video store, you can say, "Do you want a recommendation for a good movie to rent?"

If you see someone carrying a tennis racket, you could say something like: "Excuse me, but could you recommend a good place to take tennis lessons?" or "Do you know a good place to play without having to wait for a court?" or "I notice you have a racket like the one I'm interested in buying. How do you like it?" or "I see you're a tennis player. I want to start playing. Can you recommend a good racket for a beginner?"

Icebreaker #2: Make a Positive or Lighthearted Comment

Is commenting on the weather trite? Apparently Mark Twain, the great American author, didn't think so. As he stood under a store awning, waiting for a sudden downpour to end, the fellow beside him remarked, "What a storm! I wonder if it will ever stop." Twain responded, "It always has before." He also added, "Everybody talks about the weather but nobody does anything about it."

Commenting on the weather is probably the most common way to break the ice, and why not? Is it clever or insightful? Does it show how creative and witty you are? Probably not, but who cares? And to those people who claim that breaking the ice by commenting on the weather is boring, you're missing the point. If you want to send a signal to someone that you are willing to talk and want to make contact, a comment to a stranger on a hot day such as "What are you doing to stay looking so cool on such a hot day?" will usually do the trick.

Your Comments Reveal How You See the World Around You

Spontaneously commenting to someone about what you both observe is a way of instantly sharing an experience that can easily lead to more conversation. The trick to extending a brief comment into a chat is to follow it with light, upbeat remarks—not complaints or grim views. Because this method of breaking the ice reveals how you see the world, others will assume that you will see them in a negative way if your comments tend toward the negative. That's why complaining rarely leads to extended conversations. On the other hand, lighthearted comments reveal your sense of humor and make you appear friendly and appealing to talk to.

For example, if you are attending a concert, you can say to the person seated next to you, "This band is great! I wish I were a rock star!" Or if you are in the company cafeteria waiting to pay for lunch, you can comment, "I can't believe the size of these sandwiches! I could chew on one of these for days!"

A Bit of Wit Can Turn a Mundane Comment into a Funny Remark

There's no question that a quick wit facilitates conversation. For example, a friend of mine was on his way out of a wine store and was walking a few feet behind a woman who had her little dog in tow. "Come on, Shakespeare, it's time to go home and have dinner," she said to the pup. Once outside the store, my friend casually remarked to the woman, "So that's the dog who wrote all those plays." The woman chuckled and they engaged in a short conversation about wine and pets.

Hint: Keep your ears open for what other people say and make a comment that shows your wit and sense of humor. Making people laugh is always a winner in beginning conversations.

Icebreaker #3: Offer a Sincere Compliment

Everyone loves to be complimented, and it's a great way to break the ice. First, notice something interesting about the person you wish to speak with and, in a friendly and sincere manner, give him or her a compliment. Quickly following up with a related closed-ended question makes it easy for the person to offer a short reply. Plus, answering a question can reduce the embarrassment some people feel when they get a compliment from a stranger. Your kind words tell

A compliment followed by an easy-to-answer ritual question is a good way to break the ice.

the other person that you see him or her in a positive way and that you want to engage in a conversation related to that topic.

For example:

- **To a colleague you've never met, you could say:** "I see you dressed so nicely every day and just wanted to say I love your clothes! Do you mind if I ask you where you shop?"

- **To someone standing in a line waiting at a bank or store, you could say:** "That's a beautiful bracelet you're wearing! What kind of stone is it?"

- **To someone at a fitness center, you could say:** "You're in terrific shape! What kind of exercise program do you use?"

- **To someone walking a dog, you could say:** "What a beautiful dog! What kind is it?"

- **To someone new at work, you could say:** "I saw your first presentation yesterday and enjoyed it! Where did you work before you came here?"

- **To someone dressed to the nines, you could say:** "You look stunning in that outfit! Are you going someplace special?"

Here are a few dos and don'ts about giving compliments:

- **Do** keep compliments brief and sincere.
- **Don't** go overboard or gush.
- **Do** compliment others on how they look, what they say, and what they do.
- **Don't** make your compliments overly personal (unless you know the person well).
- **Don't** keep repeating the same compliment.
- **Do** follow your compliment with a related question.

Here are a few dos and don'ts about receiving compliments:

- **Do** accept a compliment gracefully. Say, "That's nice of you to say so."
- **Don't** diminish a compliment by saying, "Really, you think this old rag looks great?"
- **Do** smile and say, "Thank you."
- **Don't** assume that the person offering you a compliment wants something in return.
- **Do** acknowledge the person's positive comment with, "Thanks. I'm glad you like it."

FAQ
I'm at a cocktail party, and I don't know anyone. It seems like everybody knows everybody else except me. How do I go up to someone and start a conversation?

Starting conversations at a party is easier if you first take a little extra time to prepare mentally. Scan a few current magazines and newspapers for unusual or interesting stories. Look for any news items that may be of interest to other guests you know will be at the party. In addition, write a short list of events going on in your life that you are willing to share with others. Remember, the more conversational "fuel" you bring to the party, the easier it will be to break the ice and get a conversation going.

When you enter the room, look for friendly faces among the crowd and for people talking. You might assume that people are old buddies just because they are having a lively chat, but often they have met mere minutes before, so don't assume you're the only outsider. Use plenty of eye contact, smile, and, above all, keep your arms uncrossed and your hands away from your face. Begin to circulate around the room, observing the people as you travel to the food table, bar, or central area where people are congregating and talking. Keep your eyes open for friends, acquaintances, or people already engaged in a conversation that appears open to others. Then casually stroll over and (using their names, if you remember) say, "Hi, how are you?" or "Well, hello! It's been a while. How have you been?" or "Hello, my name is . . ." or "Hi, didn't we meet at . . . ? My name is . . ." Remember, what you say is less important than sending body language signals that say you want to communicate.

When you meet a complete stranger at a party, the easiest way to break the ice is to introduce yourself and say how you know the host. In most cases, the other person will reciprocate. Listen carefully for any words that may suggest a common interest or connection. For example, perhaps you both work for the same business or live in the same neighborhood, but never had the opportunity to formally meet. You can also comment about the food, the music, the pictures on the walls, or anything or anyone in your immediate surroundings—as long as it is positive! Here are some opening lines that will come in handy at a cocktail party:

- **To someone beside you at the food table:** "I'm wondering, do you have any idea what ingredients are in this appetizer? It's fantastic!"

- **To someone tapping her foot to the music:** "You look like you're really enjoying this music. Me too. Do you want to dance?"

- **To someone who obviously spent extra effort to look really snazzy:** "Excuse me, but I couldn't help but notice what an attractive scarf you have on. How did you come up with such an unusual way to tie it?"

- **To someone standing alone after a business-related party:** "Hello. My name is . . . Actually, I'm a new member in this organization. What did you think of tonight's speaker?"

- **To someone admiring an antique or knickknack:** "I love all these old toys and odds and ends. I think our host must like to go to garage sales and flea markets as much as I do. I wonder why so many people love to collect the strangest things."

- **To someone dancing:** "Excuse me, but you sure look great out there on the dance floor. Would you show me a few steps?"

Icebreaker #4: Introduce Yourself

Introducing yourself and following it with a comment or question is a natural and easy way to break the ice and start conversations at social and business events or in your neighborhood. Taking the initiative to break the ice by introducing yourself shows you are confident and want to connect with others.

A Pause Is the Perfect Time to Introduce Yourself

When is the best time to introduce yourself? Generally, the longer you wait to introduce yourself, the more uncomfortable people seem to get. The sooner you take the initiative, the better. When there is a pause in conversation, that is a good time to say, "By the way, my name is . . . What's yours?" The other person will almost certainly respond in kind. Offer a handshake and a friendly smile, repeat the person's name, and say, "Nice to meet you." (For more on this subject see chapter 5, "Mastering the Art of Remembering Names.") Next, ask a question or make a comment about what the other person has told you, and your conversation will be off and running.

As with other icebreakers, keep your comments positive and your questions straightforward and easy to answer. Here are some examples:

- **At a party:** "Hello, my name's . . . I'm an old friend of our host. What about you?"

- **At a networking event:** "How do you do? My name's . . . How do you like the program so far?"

- **At a business meeting:** "Hello, I'd like to introduce myself. My name is . . . I work in the . . . department. Are you with our company?"

- **In your neighborhood:** "Hi, I live around the corner. My name is . . . What's yours?"

A Few Hints about Dealing with Rejection When Breaking the Ice

Minimize Rejections: Look for Receptivity

The more you practice breaking the ice and starting conversations, the better responses you will get. Of course, there are going to be some rejections, too. No one receives unanimous approval, so when you are rejected, don't dwell on it. Instead, use it as a lesson and adjust your approach for the next time.

The best way to minimize rejection is to look for receptivity in those you approach. Try to be sensitive to "where others are at." Look for open arms, eye contact, and a smile. Look for people who are sending receptive signals through their body language and, when you feel the time is right, approach them in a friendly and direct way.

For example, if you are at a party or singles event and would like to ask someone for a dance, look to those who are dancing or look as if they want to dance. Wait for a new song to start playing and then take the risk. Move closer to the person and establish eye contact, smile, and ask the person for a dance. Chances are she will feel flattered that you have noticed her and hopefully will accept your invitation. If, however, the answer is no, then accept it gracefully with a smile ("like water off a duck's back") and ask someone else. Keep asking and you're bound to get an acceptance. The more you ask, the better you'll become at picking out people who will respond the way you want them to.

A Philosophical Look at Rejections When Breaking the Ice

If you're rejected when reaching out to people, don't automatically assume it's your fault. The other person may have several reasons for not responding the way you want, none of which may have anything to do with you. Perhaps the person is busy, waiting for someone else, or just shy. Rejections are a part of everyday life. Don't let them keep you from trying to start conversations with others. When you begin to get encouraging responses, then you are on the right track. It's all a matter of numbers and your conversation skills. Count the positive responses and forget about the rejections.

This simple philosophy can help people who fear rejection start more conversations. If you have only taken a few risks to break the ice and have been rejected once or twice, then those rejections may loom large. If, on the other hand, you take more risks and start conversations, you will receive a mixture of open and closed responses, and each rejection will become less and less meaningful. Focus on the positive responses and you will get better at choosing receptive people. You really have very little to lose—and a lot to gain. Taking the risk to be the first to say hello isn't such a fearful step. When you take the active role, you are sending this message: "I'm friendly and willing to communicate if you are."

Knowing What to Say Next
by Listening

The cure for boredom is curiosity. There is no cure for curiosity.
—Dorothy Parker (1893–1967), American author, poet, critic

Okay, you've broken the ice by asking some ritual questions, making a few light comments, and introducing yourself. Hopefully, the other person responded with a few ritual questions and comments so you know that he or she is willing to communicate. But how can you turn a few remarks into a real conversation that lasts more than a minute? What can you say next to get the conversation going?

Listening for Key Words Is the Secret to Continuing Conversations

The secret to knowing what to say after you break the ice is to listen carefully for key words beginning from the moment you say hello, including topics, facts, opinions, feelings, and experiences. Listening for key words and responding to them with follow-up questions and relevant comments are the secrets to growing conversations. Many people are so preoccupied with thinking, *Oh, no, it's going to be my turn to talk soon, and I won't know what to say!* that they don't hear what the other person is saying. So don't worry about what you are going to say next, because while you are thinking, you're not listening!

Use and Listen for "Key Words"

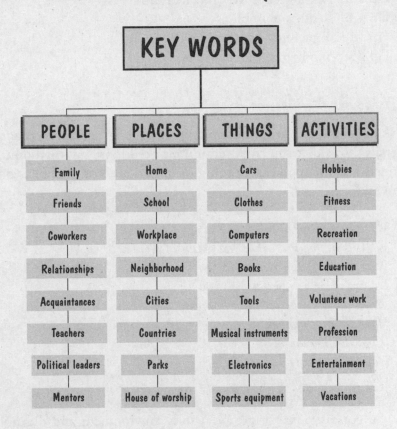

Five Tips to Tune Up Your Listening Skills

Comedian and author Fran Lebowitz once joked, "The opposite of talking isn't listening, it's waiting." Everyone has been guilty at one time or another of tuning out instead of listening while another person speaks. But poor listening can damage more than your conversations: it can scuttle your career and relationships. However, you can improve your listening skills in any conversation if you follow these tips:

Tip #1: Ask clarification questions.
Tip #2: Acknowledge free information.
Tip #3: Request examples.
Tip #4: Tune in to what's *not* said.
Tip #5: Summarize the main points.

Tip #1: Ask Clarification Questions

Asking follow-up clarification questions for more specific facts and details shows that you are listening but need more information to understand the speaker's meaning or intentions. For example, you can ask:

What do you mean when you say . . . ?
What is it about . . . that you think is so great?
Why do you feel so . . . about that?
Do you mean to say that . . . ?
When do you expect that to happen?
How did that happen?
What did you do next?
How did it turn out?
Who said what to whom?

If you got distracted or are in a noisy environment and did not clearly hear what the other person said—or you want a few extra seconds to consider your response—you can say, "I'm sorry, I missed what you just said. Can you please repeat what you just told me?"

Tip #2: Acknowledge Free Information

When we communicate with one another, we reveal much more than we realize. The information that we volunteer is called *free information*, and it's usually what we want to talk about when we are chatting with someone. You show you are listening when you ask a person questions based on their free information. Most people feel important and flattered when you listen to them and respond to what they've said. It also makes them like you and increases your rapport with them. Acknowledging the information a person volunteers to you will encourage him or her to open up and offer even more topics for the two of you to talk about. For example, you can say:

> *You just said something that I think is really interesting. Why . . . ?*
> *I gather from what you just told me that you . . . What is it that makes you say that?*
> *Since you brought up the fact that . . . , can I ask you . . . ?*
> *I would have never guessed that you . . . Thanks for letting me know that.*

Tip #3: Request Examples

Ask for and offer examples that support or question what is being said. If you are not sure what the other person is saying, or you don't understand what she is talking about, ask for an example to make the point clear for you. You can ask:

> *Like what, for instance?*
> *What would that include?*
> *How will I know?*
> *Can you describe your idea of a good . . . for me?*
> *How would you describe it?*

Tip #4: Tune In to What's Not Said

Tuning in to what people *don't say* but *imply* is as important as listening to the words they speak. To understand a person's implied messages, you need to listen carefully between the lines of conversation for what I call "iceberg" statements. An iceberg statement is a comment or a piece of free information where 90 percent is under the surface, waiting to be asked about. Iceberg statements usually come in the form of one or two words that accompany answers to ritual questions. These statements are hints about topics that people really want to talk about if they think you might be interested. For example, when you hear someone say something like "You'll never believe what happened to me . . ." or "Guess what

Iceberg Statements Send This Message: "Ask Me More"

Listen for "Iceberg Statements"

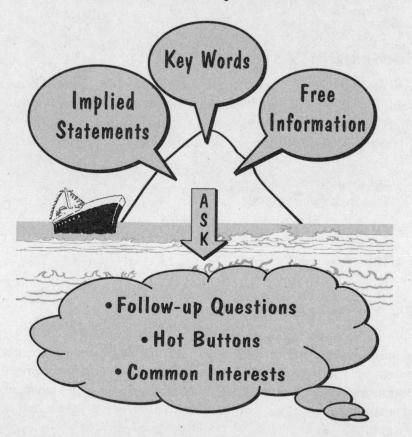

I've been doing?" they are sending you a message that they want to talk more about the topic. When you hear an iceberg statement, quickly ask a related follow-up question or say: "What happened?" or "You don't say! Tell me, how was it?" or "Why do you say that?" or "In what ways?" or "How so?"

Also listen for iceberg statements that point to an iceberg topic; for example:

> *My grandkids are visiting this weekend.*
> *I'm going to a foreign film tonight with some people from my language class.*
> *I hope the weather is good this weekend.*
> *I'm thinking about some career training in . . .*

Tip #5: Summarize the Main Points

It is not uncommon for people talking to wander off the main topic. When you are listening, it is helpful to keep the main theme in mind and, from time to time, to summarize what the other person has said. You can say something like "It sounds to me like you are saying . . . Am I right?" This focuses your listening skills and helps you remember important details and the main ideas of the conversation. When you understand a person's main point, restate it. For example, you can say:

> *If I understand you correctly, you want to . . .*
> *Let me see if I've got this straight. You're going to . . . Is that right?*
> *So your main point is . . . Am I correct?*

Conversations Are More Fun When You Actively Listen

Listen actively in every conversation. By participating with questions and comments, you'll improve your listening skills and retention of details and main ideas. Plus, the other person will feel more comfortable because you're showing interest in what he or she has been talking about. Be sure to link the new information with your prior knowledge and experience. Ask yourself: *How does what he or she just said relate to my understanding and experience of the topic?* Combining your prior knowledge and new information will provide you with enough new questions and comments to easily continue the conversation.

FAQ

How can I get others to be more open to what I have to say?

One way to get a person to consider your ideas or views is to first ask for his or her opinion on the topic and then listen. For example, you can ask, "Can I get your opinion on something I've been thinking about for a while? How do you feel about . . . ?" Not only does this make the person feel important, but it also gives you a sense of how receptive he or she may be to your idea. Then you can say, "That's interesting you say that, because here is what I'm thinking and I'd like to get your feedback on this." By first listening to the other person's viewpoint, you will be projecting your own receptivity and, as a result, increase his or her openness to your ideas.

Good Listening Requires Practice and Concentration

Active listening skills need to be practiced. As you become more adept at listening, your conversational abilities will improve. By listening and asking tuned-in questions, the other person will feel more comfortable opening up to you. When you share a person's enthusiasm for a topic by listening closely to what he or she says, you are giving a green light to continue. Active listening sends this message: "I'm interested in what you are saying: Keep talking, I want to hear more!"

Telling Others Who You Are

I tell ya when I was a kid, all I knew was rejection. My yo-yo—
it never came back.
  —Rodney Dangerfield (1921–2004), American actor and comic

Do you maintain a veil of privacy because you believe that: (1) if people knew what you were really like, they would think less of you? (2) being too familiar with someone breeds contempt, so remaining mysterious is best? (3) if a person knew intimate or personal facts about you, he or she might use this information against you?

Yes, it's wise to be prudent about what you disclose to the people you've just met. However, if you are overly guarded, you will leave the impression that you have something to hide. A good conversation consists of more than people asking questions and making comments. If you listen carefully to a conversation between two people who are getting to know each other, you'll hear both parties revealing pieces of personal information that fill in the pictures of who they are. These revelations, called *self-disclosures*, take place during all stages of a relationship but are essential during the first few minutes of a conversation as the people determine whether or not they want to get to know each other better.

Self-Disclosure Lets People Get to Know You on Your Own Terms

No one expects (or wants) you to reveal your deepest fears or secrets, but if you desire meaningful conversations, be prepared to reveal some of your history and what is important to you, a little at a time. The information you disclose determines how others get to know you—and it's all up to you what you reveal. Be enthusiastic when you share your interests and gradually tell others about your background, family, goals, what you do for work, and, most important, your "hot buttons," or passions. (For more about hot buttons, see chapter 6.) However, it's best to keep disclosures related to your health, finances, family difficulties, and work or legal problems to yourself until you know the person better.

Telling Others What You Do for a Living

Some people feel uncomfortable if others ask them the ritual question "What do you do?" They feel people will stereotype them or make assumptions based on how they earn a living. No one likes being put into a pigeonhole, but if you get annoyed or become resistant when asked what you do, you'll throw cold water on the conversation. Although I don't recommend it as a good first question to ask when you meet someone, it's useful to be ready with a short answer if asked.

If you like talking about your occupation, then reveal some free information and see if the other person shows more interest. After a few sentences about your line of work, it's fine to ask what he or she does for a living. For example, you can say, "Now you know a little about what I do for work. What about you?" If, however, you prefer not to discuss your work, still answer the question in a few words. Then add free information about what you *do* want to talk about. For example, you might say, "To pay the bills I work as a . . . , but my real passion is . . . !" You can then reveal other basic information and guide the direction of the conversation to your preferred topic.

If the other person has told you how he earns a living and you insist on keeping your means of support a secret, he will probably become suspicious or lose interest in trying to get to know you. After all, if you hope to make friends with people, how long can you withhold this basic information?

Many people who don't like to tell others what they do for a living are also anxious about other types of ritual background questions. They feel this kind of information is dull and boring and should be avoided. Instead, they say they want to talk about deep and meaningful topics that allow them to expound on their values and beliefs. The fact is, conversations that do not go through the ritual phases of self-disclosure rarely proceed to deeper and more meaningful levels.

Realistically, What Do You Have to Lose?

Once you take a look at what is being revealed, the details aren't secrets that must be kept. Close and meaningful relationships are nearly impossible without some personal revelations and feelings of mutual trust and confidence. Trust is created by being willing to reveal some personal information to the other person. While some feelings and personal history are best kept to oneself, especially in work-related situations, it can be destructive to let an overly guarded attitude carry over into your personal life. Although there are some who do take unfair advantage of others' personal disclosures, most people consider it a sign of trust. So the next time someone asks you a personal question about your background, offer a self-disclosure that reveals a little more of who you are. It will lead to deeper conversations and more personal relationships. Remember, you don't have to give an in-depth analysis of your life—just show the tip of the iceberg.

Four Levels of Self-Disclosure That Lead to Better Relationships

There are four levels of self-disclosure; the first three we generally use when we meet people and chat for the first few times. They are: ritual greetings, background facts, and opinions and preferences. The fourth level of self-disclosure—deeper feelings and personal experiences—should be reserved for someone you know better and can trust with more personal revelations.

Level 1: Ritual Greetings Reveal Receptivity and Availability for Conversations

The first level of self-disclosure is a ritual greeting. These are very general disclosures and are responses to ritual greetings such as: "How are you?" "What's new?" "How are you doing?" "How have you been?" and "How's the family?" Although these questions usually evoke responses such as "Fine!" and "Great!" you might also hear less cheerful answers such as "Not bad" and "I've been better." Either way, these low-level disclosures provide an excellent opportunity to gauge the level of receptivity and willingness of the speaker to participate in a conversation.

Level 2: Basic Background Information Reveals Where You Are From and What You Do

After people exchange greetings, they usually exchange some basic personal facts. Intersperse in your conversation what you do for work and fun, where you are from, where you went to school, where you have lived, some family history and mention of nationality, what your hobbies are, and some current projects or activities that you are involved in or passionate about. This second level of self-disclosure provides information for conversational partners to compare and explore. It is at this point that people begin to get to know each other. This is the area of conversation where people most often find that they have something in common.

For example, to disclose a snapshot of your family background you can say something like "I was born and raised in . . . along with an older sister. My mother was born and raised in . . . My father's family came from . . ."

Disclose your hopes, dreams, loves, joys, and sorrows so people will be able to identify with you. We all share these basic emotional experiences.

Level 3: Preferences and Opinions Reveal Your Values and Attitudes

The third level of self-disclosure is revealing personal opinions and preferences on different subjects. At this level you can reveal your attitudes, values, and concerns. You can tell others what you honestly think and feel about the world around us. Express your ideas in an open manner and encourage others to share their ideas on varied topics. In general, most people prefer others who are like-minded. Disclosing your preferences, opinions, goals, hopes, and dreams allows you to identify and connect with those people. For example, to tell others about a longtime goal or dream, you can say something like "It's always been my dream to . . . and now that's what I'm going to do," "I've been working for years to . . . and I'm nearly finished!" or "I'm doing something now that I've wanted to do for a long time, and that is . . ."

However, remember not to be strident when expressing your political or religious views. For example, to disclose your political beliefs, you can say, "I belong to the . . . Party," or "I always base my vote on the candidate, not the party." To disclose your religious beliefs, you can say, "Regarding my religion, I was raised a . . . These days I worship at . . ." or "I don't belong or subscribe to any particular religion."

Some people refrain from expressing their views because the don't want to offend or sound opinionated. While you don't want to make overly strong statements, not expressing your views or saying "It doesn't matter to me" creates the impression that you don't care or that you lack the confidence to state your opinion. Expressing opinions and preferences allows people an opportunity to get to know more about one another on a more meaningful level.

For example, you can say, "I see the situation this way . . . How do you see it?" or "When it comes to . . . I prefer to . . . What about you?"

Level 4: Feelings and Personal Experiences Reveal Sensitive Topics, Deeper Feelings, and Meaningful Experiences

The final level of self-disclosure concerns your personal feelings about people, events, and personal experiences that have had an impact on your life—for better or worse. These are the most difficult disclosures we make because they require us to reveal our emotions and sensitive topics. Though it can be difficult—and risky—to show your feelings and talk about particular personal experiences, it will give people a more meaningful sense of who you are and what is important to you. When you disclose your fears, hopes, dreams, loves, joys, and sorrows, people will be able to identify with you, because we all share these basic emotional experiences.

For example, you can say, "When I was . . . I was scared to death that I was going to . . ." or "I have strong feelings about that topic because . . ." or "That's an issue I've experienced firsthand, and I can tell you, it wasn't easy to deal with."

Do not reveal overly personal feelings, opinions, or experiences without going through the other levels of self-disclosure and establishing a comfortable level of rapport and mutual trust. However, it is important not to make your conversation a therapy session. Also, many people make the common mistake of using the word *you* when they mean *I*. These are your disclosures, so be sure to preface them with the words "I feel (think, want, etc.) . . ."

Hints about Self-Disclosures

Most people are curious about one another and have a desire for at least some casual and personal contact. When you share aspects of your life with another person, you are making this all-important contact with her. However, keep these two points in mind:

- **Offer your self-disclosures a little at a time.** Offering too many self-disclosures at one time can overwhelm a listener. We've all experienced someone telling us in excruciating detail his or her life story—and we know how uncomfortable and, often, boring this can be. Your conversations will flow much better with the people you meet when you reveal your background and experiences a little at a time and within the context of the situation you are in.

   For example, if you are attending a wedding reception, you could reveal to a person with whom you are chatting,

"I've been married (divorced) for . . . years," or "I'm still looking for the right person," or "My idea of a good marriage is . . ."

- **Present a genuine picture of yourself.** Do you remember meeting someone who tried hard to show how smart, talented, or successful he was? Did he make a positive impact, or were you less than impressed? If you boost or exaggerate your good qualities, people will soon realize that you are not presenting a real picture of who you are. Likewise, first meetings are not the time to disclose your peccadilloes or personal failures. Instead, disclose some of the challenges and details of what brought you to where you are today. This will tell people you meet who you are without making it sound like you are bragging or saying, "This is who I am—warts and all."

FAQ

How do you gracefully tell someone she is asking questions that are too personal?

Generally, it's considered rude to ask overly personal questions about money, health, or relationships when you first meet someone, but some people do. Don't be surprised if it happens, just be ready to respond. If you are asked a question you'd rather not answer, simply say, "I'd rather not answer that, if you don't mind." Most people will accept this statement as a courteous way of saying, "Mind your own business." If you are asked how much something costs and you'd rather not discuss it, say, "I don't really know because it was a gift," or you can say with a wink, "Probably too much (or not enough)!"

It is your right to decline to answer any question that you feel is too personal. However, after declining, it's up to you to throw the conversational ball back to the other person with a question or change the topic.

Telling Others Who You Are Facilitates Personal Connections

The degree to which you exchange meaningful information directly affects how well you connect with the people you meet. As your exchanges progress through the four levels of self-disclosure, you'll not only be getting to know one another on your own terms, you'll be setting the stage for longer and more meaningful conversations.

Mastering the Art of Remembering Names

> Most people are too conscious of their own problems in this
> matter to hold yours against you. Even if they wanted to give you
> a black mark, they wouldn't know next to whose name to put it.
> —Judith Martin, a.k.a. "Miss Manners" (1938–),
> author, etiquette expert

Five Seconds Is All the Time It Takes to Make a Great First Impression

Five seconds! That's all the time it takes to introduce yourself and remember a person's name. Five seconds! What faster way is there to begin a successful business or social relationship?

The famous author and public speaker Dale Carnegie said, "The sweetest sound in any language is a person's name." There's no question about it. People feel flattered when you remember their names. When you remember the name of a person you've recently met, you make him feel important and special and you add a large measure of personal warmth and friendliness to the conversation. Remembering names also shows that you are listening, builds rapport with new acquaintances, and helps overcome the natural barriers that separate strangers.

Do You Want to Improve Your Ability to Remember Names?

How many times have you been talking to someone you've met before—maybe even more than once—and you can't remember his name? Or you're introducing mutual friends or acquaintances, and one person's name just slips right out of your head? Or you go to a party and you are introduced to someone, and five seconds later you can't recall her name? Or maybe you see a client and you don't remember his name, so it's difficult to introduce him to your boss? As a result of your poor memory for names, you feel embarrassed and avoid people you already know as well as new acquaintances because you might offend them by forgetting their names.

If you answered yes to any of these questions, you're not alone. When I ask people in my networking programs who has trouble remembering the names of the people they meet, nine out of ten people raise their hands. Yes, a good memory for names is rare. However, you can learn this valuable networking and socializing skill, and it's easier than you might think!

Why Do We Forget People's Names?

The most common reason for forgetting names is failing to focus on the moment of introduction, so you never hear them in the first place. You are too busy thinking about what you're going to say next or worrying about what others will think of you. This counterproductive self-talk sounds like this: "What am I going to say after I say hello?" "Does my hair look okay?" "I don't want to be too forward." "I'm sure I'll say something stupid." "I hope I'm making a good impression." "I wonder if . . ."

Other distractions, such as loud music or people talking, can also cause you to miss the name. But lack of interest is the worst reason for failing to focus on someone's name. If you say to yourself, *I'll probably never see this person again, so why should I bother learning his name?* you have set the stage for a disjointed, impersonal, and short conversation.

Five Seconds to Success

Remember the Names of the People You Meet

Use the following five-second strategy to remember first names:

- 🕐 **The first second:** Focus on the moment of introduction.
- 🕑 **The second second:** Don't think about what to say—listen for the name.
- 🕒 **The third second:** Repeat the name aloud.
- 🕓 **The fourth second:** Think of someone you know with the same name.
- 🕔 **The fifth second:** Use the name during and at the end of the conversation.

The First Second: Focus on the Moment of Introduction

Let the other person know that you consider her name important by giving her your full attention when you are introduced. Make direct eye contact, offer a warm smile, and extend a firm, friendly handshake. Holding on to the other person's hand an extra second can help you focus on the critical moment of introduction and what is about to come next: her name.

The Second Second: Don't Think about What to Say—Listen for the Name

This is the moment you've been waiting for, so don't blow it by thinking about yourself and what you're going to say next. Concentrate your complete attention and listen for every letter in the person's name, particularly the first initial. If you missed the name, simply say, "Sorry, I didn't catch your name," or "Excuse me, I missed your name." If the name is unusual or a foreign name, or if you're still not sure what he has said, ask: "Can you spell your name for me? I want to be sure to get it right."

The Third Second: Repeat the Name Aloud

Since many names sound similar, be sure to repeat the name to make sure that you got it right. For example, you can say, "I want to make sure I have your name right. Is it Marie or Maria?" or "Your name is Pat? That's my best friend's name!" Quickly imagine the first initial etched on the person's forehead or connect it with a feature on his face. This may sound weird, but it works, especially when you are trying to recall the name later.

Repeating the name also has several additional benefits. First, it lets the other person know that you listened and that you are making a concentrated effort to remember her name. This is flattering. Second, if you got the name wrong, it allows the other person to correct you. Finally, by repeating the name, you think it, say it, and then hear it again, thus giving yourself three more repetitions in addition to hearing the name the first time. And, as most memory experts agree, repetition is one of the key ingredients to retention and recall—or, put another way: "Practice makes perfect."

The Fourth Second: Think of Someone You Know with the Same Name

Just think of all the people you know named John, Susan, Robert, Diane, Linda, Steve, Mary, or Frank. Chances are good that when you meet someone new, he or she will have the same name as someone you already know, and this will help you remember the name. As you are introduced, think of someone else you know with the same name: a relative, classmate, or even a pet! It's best to lock in on the first person who comes to mind and to use that same person each time you meet someone new with that name.

For example, each time you meet a new Barbara, always think of Aunt Barbara. The two people don't need to look anything alike. And you don't even need to actually know them personally. The name could belong to a movie star or someone you've heard of (or even a cartoon character) but don't know personally. For example, when you meet an Elizabeth, you may think of Elizabeth Taylor or Queen Elizabeth. Michael Jordan may be the first Michael you think of when you meet someone with that name, and so on. This technique may sound strange, but with a little practice, you'll remember most of your new acquaintances with common first names.

The Fifth Second: Use the Name during and at the End of the Conversation

"Pat, when you said that you . . ." "Sam, what made you decide to . . . ?" "Eileen, it was really great hearing about your trip to . . ." "Wendy, how can I get in touch with you?" Using a person's name personalizes the conversation as it reinforces your memory and ability to recall it at your next meeting. Ending the conversation with her name leaves a great first impression and completes the cycle of starting, continuing, and ending a conversation.

The Trick to Remembering Names in a Group

Nearly everyone has been in the situation where there is barely enough time to shake hands with one person before being introduced to someone else. In many cases, there is less than a second or two between introductions. How can you possibly remember everyone's name? It's easy! If you focus on the moment of introduction to each person and then make a "letter chain," you will be able to remember everyone in the group.

Here's how letter chains work. English is filled with many abbreviations, acronyms, company logos using letters, and short words. The trick is to take the first letter of each person's name and quickly hook them together into an abbreviation, a letter logo, a short word, or a series of letters. The chances are good that if you can remember one or two of the names, you can use the letter chain to help recall the other people's names too.

For example, let's say you are at a party and you are introduced to George and Maria. Think *GM*, as in General Motors, or *MG*, as in the English sports car. If you remember George's name, and you remember *GM* or *MG*, that's probably all you'll need to help you recall Maria's name. Suppose you are seated around a table in a restaurant and you're introduced to Theresa, Alba, and Gary. The letter chain is a short word: *T-A-G*. Look for letter combinations such as brands, logos, abbreviations, call letters of television or radio stations, double letters (they could be the same names), or letters next to each other in the alphabet. For example, Alan, Barbara, and Carlos = *A-B-C*; Pamela, Harold, and Della = *P-H-D*; Christine, Nancy, and Nick = *C-N-N*; Peter and Pat = *P-P*; Steve and Tom = *S-T*.

To remember their names, just link the people together, even if they are not sitting or standing next to each other. Letters can be combined in any sequence that helps you give an order to the names and triggers recall. During a free moment, repeat the letters and their corresponding names to yourself a few more times. The more you repeat the names, the stronger they will stick in your mind. If you can think of a better association to fit the group of names, then make it.

Alternate Methods for Remembering Names

A note before you begin making name associations: Don't worry or edit yourself if you think of an unflattering or even downright insulting word association with the person's name. Most people won't ask you how you remembered their names; they'll just feel flattered that you did. If someone does ask, you can simply say, "You really impressed me!" Here are five more ways to remember the names of the people you meet.

"Rhymes with . . ." Associating a word that rhymes with the name is a fun way to help you recall someone you've just met. For example: Tall or Small Paul, Curly Shirley, Curt the Flirt, Handy Sandy/Andy, Fancy Nancy, Dan the Man, Silly Billy, Witty Kitty, and so on.

First names that sound like action words. Some names sound like physical movements, motions, or gestures. Here are a few examples: Phillip, as in Fill Up my gas tank. Eileen, as in I Lean on a post. Carol, as in Christmas Carol. Bob, as in Bobbing for apples. Rob, as in Robber.

First names that sound like objects. Some first names are the same as objects or words that we see and use every day. Jack, Bell, Rose, Iris, Bill, Jean, Ray, Barry (bury), Art, Angel, Bea (bee), Hope, May, and June are examples of this.

First names with the same initial as a personal interest. The first letter of some first names corresponds to the first initial of the person's interest. For example, Greg the Guitarist, Ruth the Runner, Terry the Teacher, Sally the Sailor, and Eleanor the Engineer.

Choose a feature and associate it with the name. Here's another way to remember a name. Look at the person's face carefully, and chances are you will see that one feature stands out. It may be her eyes, nose, ears, chin, forehead, brows, birthmark, or hair—or even the shape of her face. For example, Julie's big, sparkling eyes make you think of Jewel Julie. Sam's knitted brow makes him look sad, so you think Sad Sam. Frank's heavy eyebrows remind you of two Coney Island hot dogs, so you think Frankfurter Frank. Tim's slim frame makes you think of Tiny Tim.

Sandy's black hair makes you think of the black sand beach in Hawaii, so you think Black-Hair-Like-Sand Sandy. Some other possibilities are Bushy-Bearded Bill, Muscular Mark, Large Larry, Blue-Eyed Betty, Blond Barbara, Slim Jim, Hairy Barry, and so on.

FAQ

When I'm at parties, I frequently see people whom I have met before, but I can't remember their names. What can I do to avoid being put into the extremely embarrassing position of having to say, "I've forgotten your name"?

Sometimes, no matter what you do, you simply can't come up with the person's name. Here are a few additional "guerrilla" strategies for finding out people's names:

- Ask the host or someone else to identify the guests for you
- As you are engaged in conversations, carefully listen as other guests use names
- Make quick associations right away
- If possible, peek at a guest list or seating arrangement. Seeing names in print may help you figure out who's who.

Another surefire method is to reintroduce yourself with "Hello, do you remember me? I'm Don. We met quite a while ago at . . ." In most cases, the other person will be thankful that you volunteered your name and will do likewise. If he or she doesn't, you can simply ask, "And your name again is . . . ?"

And if all else fails, you can say with a sheepish grin, "Of course I know your name, but my mind has just gone blank."

With Practice, You Can Remember Five, Ten, Twenty Names or More!

You may think it takes a long time to learn how to form associations with the people you meet. The opposite is usually true, and with practice and confidence, making associations becomes instantaneous. If you perform these mental operations all the time, your ability to learn and recall first names will improve tremendously. Then, when you see people you've met before and you use their names, they'll say, "I can't believe you remembered my name!"

Remembering Someone's Name Has a Lasting Effect

The rapport that comes from remembering someone's name makes people instantly like you. As a result, a good conversation will probably begin spontaneously, and you'll both feel good about talking to each other. But something else may happen too. Just remembering his or her name could be the start of a new frienship!

Part II

Continuing and Ending Your Conversations with Charm, Confidence, and Tact

6

Keeping the Conversation Going Strong

Form a concrete concept of what you want by verbalizing your dream and you become more eloquent in describing it.
—Les Brown (1945–), author and motivational speaker

I always ask workshop attendees to tell me their biggest challenge *after* they have broken the ice, exchanged pleasantries, and chatted for a few minutes with people they've just met. Almost always someone will say, "Keeping the conversation going strong," and most people in the audience nod their heads in agreement.

Four Keys to Sustaining Your Conversations

Sustaining conversations is easy if you know the key factors involved. Of course, good body language, displaying interest and curiosity, and being friendly and enthusiastic are essential. Here are four additional keys to sustaining conversations easily and naturally.

Key #1: Focus on the situation you are in.
Key #2: Find out about the hot buttons and big events in the other person's life.
Key #3: Balance the two-way exchange of information.
Key #4: Use small talk to navigate your conversation.

Keeping the Conversation Going

Key Words
People, places, things, and other specific details that "paint pictures" for the listener.

Free Information
Facts and details a speaker volunteers without specifically being asked.

Instructions
Step-by-step procedures to accomplish a task or objective.

Iceberg Statements
Information, feelings, or interests conveyed indirectly through implied statements or objects.

Hot Buttons
Enthusiastic topics of conversation or strong personal interests.

Common Interests
Areas of mutual experience and involvement.

Key #1: Focus on the Situation You Are In

Begin by identifying yourself in your immediate environment—that is, right in the room or place where you happen to be. Why are you here? Who else is here that you already know or want to meet? What activities take place here? How did you come to be in this place? What makes this place unusual or interesting? What can you find out about this place from someone else? What previous experiences have you had in this place? How do you feel about this place?

After you break the ice and start talking, you can extend your conversation by focusing on the various aspects of your immediate surroundings. This approach will provide you with many conversational topics to ask about or comment on.

First Talk about Where You Are, Then Expand Your Conversations to Topics Related to the Surrounding Areas

Once you focus your conversation on your immediate surroundings, it's easy to expand your topics to the next immediate environment. For example, if you're in an adult education class, then the classroom is your immediate environment. After you discuss the class itself, broaden the conversation to include the school or neighborhood where the class takes place with open-ended questions like "What made you decide to take this particular class?" or comments such as "This is my first time in this part of the city, but I love to explore new neighborhoods for antiques shops and restaurants."

Focus on the various elements of your surroundings: other classes, the campus, restaurants in the area, movie theaters, clubs, etc. As you continue, broaden your discussion to include where you live, how you travel to class, recreational areas nearby, the city, or interesting outlying areas. Once you realize the enormous amount of conversational fuel directly related to where you are and your surroundings, you'll never be at a loss for words.

Key #2: Find Out about the Hot Buttons and Big Events in the Other Person's Life

Dale Carnegie wrote in his self-help classic *How to Win Friends and Influence People* that if you find the really big events in a person's life—what I call his or her hot buttons—then conversation won't be a problem. Hot buttons are areas of keen interest that you or your conversational partner can really get into and talk about for an extended period of time. Hot buttons can be work, a new job, a hobby, a career goal, an upcoming trip, a sporting activity, personal dedication to a social cause, and even a pet! Hot buttons are subjects or activities that really interest people. A hot button can be a lifelong pursuit, a passing fancy, or a current fascination—whatever turns you on!

"Hot Buttons" Are High-Interest Topics

It's important to find other people's hot buttons as soon as possible because these strong interests are extremely fertile areas for sustained conversations. The sooner you find the other person's hot buttons and reveal your own, the more energetic and stimulating conversations you'll have—and you might discover that you share some strong personal interests.

One goal of asking ritual questions is to discover the other person's hot buttons. When you know someone's hot buttons, you know how to "turn him on" and you can also find out what he considers important. You can discover where he puts his time, money, and effort—that is, what he values. This is bountiful fuel for conversation, and it tells you many insightful things about the person you're speaking with.

In addition to finding out what turns a person on, search for common goals, experiences, and ideas. People often have many topics they're interested in and willing to talk about. Since we all share common interests, it's important to fish for hot buttons in others. When you find someone with hot buttons similar to yours, you'll be able to find out if he would like to share those activities and interests with you. This is where friendships begin to develop.

How to Find Someone Else's Hot Buttons

When you walk into a room full of strangers, do you say to yourself: *I don't have anything in common with the people here?* Many people think their interests are unique and that others wouldn't be interested. The opposite is usually true. Because of our accessibility to a wide range of activities, many people share common interests, goals, and life experiences. The trick is to find out about others and discover which ones you have in common.

When seeking someone's hot buttons, fish around subject areas with ritual questions. When you receive an enthusiastic response, express interest in the subject. This doesn't mean you must have a strong interest, but it helps if you can generate a medium or slight curiosity in the subject. This allows the other person an opportunity to share some important aspects of her life with you and will create positive feelings toward you. Your conversation partner will feel that you care about her and, hopefully, she will express a similar interest in you.

People often wear or carry items that suggest their hot buttons. Look for sporting equipment, books, jewelry, clothing, or anything that might provide a clue to a person's hot buttons. People participate in activities that are hot buttons. Focus on these activities by asking open-ended ritual questions, and sustaining conversations will be easy. Look for people having fun and striving for self-improvement or personal gain, and you'll be closer to finding those people's hot buttons.

Sometimes people reveal their hot buttons through iceberg statements—that is, they make a statement that reveals the tip of the conversational iceberg, and they're just waiting to be asked the particulars of an activity or project they are involved in. Listen carefully for free information and ask open-ended follow-up questions to encourage people to talk about what they're into. You can say: "That's something I've always been curious about. How did you get involved?"

If there are few visual or verbal clues to a person's hot buttons, then signal your desire to learn more about what is important to the other person by asking questions such as:

What do you like to do when you're not working?
What kinds of activities are you interested in?
Do you have any projects that you are involved in?
What kinds of hobbies do you enjoy?
Are you involved in any particular organizations?
Any big projects in progress or on the drawing board?
*Is there something that you've always wanted to do, but never
    got around to?*

How You Can Reveal Your Hot Buttons to Others

It's not enough to find the other person's hot buttons. Remember, a good conversation is balanced, so be ready to reveal your hot buttons too. By letting others know what's important to you, you are giving them an opportunity to get to know you *on your terms* and in a way that makes a good impression. When you are invited to a party or social event, it is helpful to take a personal inventory of your hot buttons—projects or future plans—and be ready to talk about them enthusiastically with those around you.

Share Your Hot Buttons

When you share your hot buttons, be as specific as possible about your involvement. Use plenty of facts, examples, dates, and places so your conversational partner has lots of free information to question you about. Your partner may not know much about the topic, but your enthusiasm will be contagious and will provide plenty of fuel for your partner to ask follow-up questions. Here are some ways to tell others about your hot buttons:

> *I'm really excited about . . .*
> *Guess what, I'm finally going to . . .*
> *I sure am looking forward to this weekend because . . .*
> *I just finished working on . . .*
> *I'm getting ready to begin a big project involving . . .*

Caution: Take care not to use jargon or technical terms when discussing topics with people who aren't familiar with your hot button. Give them an inside look at what excites you about the topic, rather than overly specific details. Avoid talking about your own hot buttons too much; it's a common pitfall. Be sensitive to how much time you devote to your hot button without hearing again from the other person. It's all right to let someone know what turns you on, but be aware that the other person may not necessarily want to hear everything you have to say about that topic. If you get go-ahead signals like several follow-up questions, then continue with a few more sentences until you sense that the conversation should return to the other person.

Key #3: Balance the Two-way Exchange of Information

If one participant discloses too much and the other discloses too little, then the conversation is unbalanced. An unbalanced conversation will make both parties uncomfortable. One might think: *I did all the talking. She just sat there like a bump on a log!* In contrast, the other person could be thinking: *He never shut up! All he talked about was himself!*

It's easy to understand why an unbalanced conversation results in a negative impression and a short conversation. In an extended conversation, the participants are aware of the two-way information exchange passing between them. They share basic personal facts, ideas, opinions, feelings, and experiences at about the same rate. This doesn't mean a tit-for-tat exchange, but rather a general balance within the context of the conversation. After the conversation concludes, they have learned quite a bit about each other.

Sustaining Your Conversation Is Like Playing a Game of Catch

In an extended conversation, first one person has the conversational ball and talks while the other person listens. Then, after a short bit, he tosses the conversation to the other person and the roles are reversed. This "toss" can be in the form of a question, a request for an opinion, or a comment from the person whose turn it is to talk. Once your partner picks up the conversational ball, he or she can carry the topic further or change topics. By tossing the conversational ball back and forth, you and the other person can chat for as long as you want, simply by sending and receiving information about each other.

Key #4: Use Small Talk to Navigate Your Conversation

Small talk often gets a bad rap. It is not meaningless or a waste of time, as some people say—in fact, quite the contrary. Small talk is a useful conversation tool because it demonstrates receptivity and indicates a desire to continue talking; allows people to explore a variety of topics and build rapport; and can be used to guide the conversation to areas of mutual interest (and away from conversational quicksand).

Friendly Small Talk Shows You Want to Continue Your Conversation

It's natural for most people to feel a little unsure of how they come across to others they meet until they get verbal and nonverbal signals that say, *You're okay. I like talking to you.* Small talk provides speakers with the opportunity to express these rapport- and confidence-building signals. If you and your conversational partner are engaging in lively small talk, the message is clear: both of you are enjoying each other's company, are interested in the discussion, and are willing to continue the conversation.

Lively Small Talk Gives You Many Conversation Topics to Choose From

Making small talk allows participants to sprinkle plenty of key words, free information, self-disclosures, and new topics into their conversation. This provides more opportunities for you and the other person to choose topics of mutual interest. This will extend your conversation because you'll have more things to talk about. Of course, some of the small-talk topics you choose may only yield a minute or two of conversation. However, by applying good listening and questioning skills, others will lead you to "conversational gold"—that is, a person's hot button.

The information you pick up during small talk can also pay off for you in later conversations. Be sure to give your chat your full attention and remember what the other person tells you so you can refer to it at another time.

Focused Small Talk Allows You to Guide the Conversations

Once you know various topics that a person likes to talk about, you can use small talk to guide the conversation to the ones that interest you the most or are the best for the situation. To guide your conversation to one particular topic, ask questions and make comments that elicit more small talk in that area. You can say something like "You mentioned a few minutes ago that . . . I'm really interested in hearing more about that."

FAQ _____

I'm lunching with a client, and I don't want to talk about business, since our morning and afternoon are concerned with that topic. How do I make interesting informal conversation during lunch?

When you are with a client, it is helpful to know something about his or her outside interests. In many cases, if you have met before, you can obtain this information through free information and your prior conversations. If this is your first contact, then doing your homework prior to a planned meeting can make a big difference when it comes to casual conversation. With a phone call or e-mail to a mutual contact or an online search you may be able to find out a few non-work-related topics of interest to your client. (See more about this topic in part III: "Navigating Online Networks to Expand Your Business, Social, and Personal Relationships.")

When you sit down to lunch, simply say, "I understand you are quite a gardener. Can you give me a few tips? I'm just a beginner," or "I read on your company's website that you are a volunteer for . . . I'd love to hear about what you're doing for that organization."

If you don't have any inside information about the person, be particularly attentive for free information. Perhaps the person will mention in passing about being in Hawaii for a business conference. You can say, "I heard you mention earlier that you were in Hawaii. What did you enjoy most about your stay in the islands?" or "Had you been there before?"

Be sure to reveal enough free information about yourself throughout the conversation so that he will know what follow-up questions to ask you. When you sense a certain topic has been talked out, then change the subject by referring to some free information revealed earlier, or offer some new information of your own. For example, you can say, "It's interesting to hear you talk about sailing, because I like it as well. In fact, I just got back from a two-week trip off the coast of California, and it was great!"

Here are some other conversation starters you can use while dining with a client:

How did you choose your line of work?
What did you do before you joined your company?
Have you ever wanted to own your own business?
What new trends do you see coming in our industry?
What do you think of . . . ? (Refer to an interesting news story.)

Changing Topics Adds Variety and Opportunity to Your Conversation

Changing topics is probably the easiest way to sustain a conversation while fishing for mutual areas of interest with your partner. You don't have to talk out one topic before proceeding to the next. Good conversations are normally an interweaving of subjects and ideas, and it's not uncommon for participants to jump from point to point. It's helpful to stay within generally related subject areas, but if your discussion proceeds into new areas, you can always return to the original topic by saying, "Getting back to what you said before about . . ."

Use Key Words to Change Topics

"I Heard You Mention Earlier . . ."

The most common method of changing topics is to refer to previously revealed free information by commenting or asking a closed-ended ritual question. For example, "I remember you mentioned earlier that you were in Hawaii last month. Were you there for business or pleasure?" Always listen carefully for any previously mentioned key words, since they can be used as a reference to restart discussion on a past topic. If the topic you've been discussing has run its course, just change the topic by inserting an open-ended ritual question based on your own or your partner's free information.

Sometimes you might want to change to another topic for only a brief moment. All you have to do is say, "Excuse me, but I'd like to change the subject for a moment," and then make your comment or ask your question. Try to complete your ideas quickly and then return to your original topic of discussion.

Caution: Be careful to maintain focus. Jumping from topic to topic can give your partner the impression that you cannot (or don't care to) discuss an issue on a meaningful level. It may also indicate that you are not listening or that you are bored with the subject matter—both of which may be true! If your partner gives you a brief response, she may not wish to discuss the topic for a particular reason. Be sensitive to unenthusiastic responses, and be ready to change to a new topic quickly when you feel you have touched on a high-sensitivity or low-interest area for the other person.

Small Talk Helps You Avoid Sinking into Conversational Quicksand

Have you been in a conversation when someone brings up an unpleasant topic such as the death of a celebrity, a gory crime, world conflicts, famine, or an environmental disaster? Or one minute you and a new acquaintance are having a friendly chat when the topic of politics or religion comes up, and the next thing you know, you're scrapping like two alley cats? If so, you know that the wrong topics can quickly turn pleasant chats sour, leaving both parties with negative impressions of each other. If you let this happen in your conversations, it will most likely inhibit or even ruin your chances for future contact. Fortunately, you can avoid this common pitfall if you use small talk to change the topic before your chat sinks into a conversational quagmire.

"Let's Change the Subject!"

It's best not to even get into discussions about subjects that are in poor taste, are "downers," or concern other unpleasant topics that make people uncomfortable. To avoid them, you'll need to change the topic. For example, just say something like "I'm sure we can find more pleasant things to talk about," or "Let's talk about something more positive," or "I hope you don't mind, but I'd rather talk about something else at the dinner table." Once you've made the suggestion to change the subject, then it's up to you to do just that. Pick up the conversational ball quickly and open a new topic of discussion by making a comment or asking an open-ended question based on free information that you heard earlier, before the conversation took an unfortunate turn. Usually the other participants within earshot will feel relieved that the negative topic didn't last too long.

Robust Conversations Build Self-confidence and Pave the Way to Relationships

Sustaining your conversation is easy when you focus on the situations you are in, share your hot buttons and upbeat topics, exchange meaningful information, and use small talk to build rapport, change topics, and guide the conversation to areas of mutual interest. When you do, you'll get to know each other better, but there's an even bigger benefit: robust conversations build self-confidence and create stronger connections that can lead to dynamic business, social, and personal relationships.

7

Dealing with Awkward Conversations

The real art of conversation is not only to say the right thing at the right place but to leave unsaid the wrong thing at the tempting moment.
—Lady Dorothy Nevill (1826–1913), British author

Do you remember the last time you felt like giving someone "a piece of your mind" but you weren't sure what to say without making matters worse? We all face awkward conversations or moments when we feel compelled to speak but want to do so tactfully. Usually a thoughtful response will decrease the uneasiness that often accompanies awkward conversations, so before you speak, give yourself a few seconds to consider how to respond with *T-A-C-T*.

T = Think Before You Speak

Taking a deep breath and considering your words before you respond to a criticism, aggressive challenge, or blunt remark serves two purposes. First, it helps you relax and think clearly by sending more oxygen to your brain. Second, it prevents knee-jerk responses that often make awkward conversations even more uncomfortable. A moment of silence is a tactful strategy that is neither a confirmation nor a denial. It allows you a few extra seconds to consider what was said, how to respond, and what you want to say.

A = Actively Listen

Actively listening means asking a few clarification questions about the other person's words, state of mind, or motives and then carefully listening for facts, feelings, and implied meanings. This tactful strategy provides you with additional information and more time to focus your response where it will do the most good—that is, getting the outcome you desire. It also allows the other person to clarify or reconsider his or her comments. To show you are listening, paraphrase what you believe the other person has told you. For example, you can say, "Let me make sure I understand what you're saying. Do you mean that . . . ?"

C = Consider the Outcome

Before you begin an awkward conversation, think about the possible outcomes and which one you want. Before speaking, first decide what you want to happen after you respond. What do you want the other person to do? For example, perhaps you want the other person to back off and stop bugging you; talk more openly about his or her expectations and needs; handle his or her own problems; help you more with chores; or take more personal responsibility.

Whatever it is, this tactful strategy of considering the outcome allows you to choose the best words and actions to achieve that result.

T = Tread Lightly

Now is the time to speak up, but do so with a light touch, because coming on too strong will more likely elicit a negative reaction. Balance an assertive response for a specific outcome with the needs of the other person. Listening to and considering the other person is a tactful strategy that can help decrease the discomfort that often accompanies awkward conversations. For example, to gently bring up an issue, you can ask, "I want to ask you a favor that would mean a lot to me. Will you please . . . ?"

Fifteen Awkward Situations and How to Respond

Here are some examples of common awkward conversations, why they are a problem, a desired outcome, and a tactful response.

Awkward Conversation 1: A Colleague Tries to Draw You into a Political Debate

> **Problem:** Discussing politics at work is a "taboo topic," and for good reason. Most people have strong opinions about emotional topics that can lead to harsh disagreements. If that happens, personal relationships, work relationships, and career opportunities can suffer.

> **Desired outcome:** Avoid a political argument and change topics.

> **Tactful response:** Don't get into this "lose-lose" conversation. Simply say: "I never discuss politics at work (parties, dinner, etc.). To change the subject, what are you doing this weekend?"

Awkward Conversation 2: A Coworker Tries to Get You to Do His Work

> **Problem:** If you let unmotivated people take advantage of your good nature and work ethics, they will.

> **Desired outcome:** Let your coworkers know that they need to pull their weight.

> **Tactful response:** "If you need extra help, maybe you want to let our supervisor know. I can't do your work and mine too."

FAQ

It never fails: at least twice a week my boss asks me to work late just about the time I'm getting ready to go home. What can I say to him to get him to stop doing this?

To deal with a boss who always pressures you to work late, it's important to be assertive, but also use common sense. After all, you still want to have a job when you arrive for work the next day. Start by stating assertively what you want while letting your boss know that you understand and sympathize with the problem. For example, the conversation might go as follows:

Boss: Diane, Jean won't be coming in, so I'm going to need you to stay late tomorrow to finish those reports.

Diane: Gee, Mr. Lund, that's impossible. I have something planned for right after work, and I can't miss it.

Boss: Well, you'll just have to change your plans or be late, because the main office wants those reports in by the next day, or it will be my neck.

Diane: I'd like to be able to help you, Mr. Lund, but I won't be able to work late tomorrow night.

Boss: You've always been so reliable before, and now you're letting me down. This is really putting me in a tough spot!

Diane: I understand that you need someone to finish the reports, but I won't be available. This is something I've been planning for a long time.

Boss: But who am I going to get to finish up those reports?

Diane: Have you thought about giving Jeff a call? He said he was looking for some extra work. Maybe he can help.

Boss: Jeff? That's an idea. He might be the solution.

Diane: Good. I'm sure Jeff would be happy to do the job.

Boss: Okay, Diane, thanks. . . . Oh, and have a good time
tomorrow night.
Diane: Thank you, Mr. Lund.

Use Tact and Common Sense When Saying No to Your Boss

Assertive conversations with your supervisor or employer require
plenty of tact and common sense. *When* you say no is as important
as *how* you say no. Although sometimes you will need to work
late, you can tell her that you won't always be available to work
overtime. For example, you can say, "I understand that on occa-
sion I'll need to work late. But I have other responsibilities, too, so
I won't be available to work past 5:00 P.M. on a regular basis."

Hopefully, by putting your boss on notice that your work time
is limited, he will make other arrangements when it's necessary.

Awkward Conversation 3: **Constant Request for Contributions to Charitable Organizations**

> **Problem:** With so many people in need these days, there
> is enormous pressure (and guilt) to help, but giving to all
> is impossible.
>
> **Desired outcome:** Get people to stop asking you for money.
>
> **Tactful response:** "I'd like to give to every worthy cause,
> but I can't: so I've narrowed my list of charities to just a
> few, and that's it."

Awkward Conversation 4: **A Relative Asks Why You Aren't Married or Don't Have Children**

> **Problem:** This comment implies disapproval of your life-
> style.
>
> **Desired outcome:** Put an end to these personal questions.
>
> **Tactful response:** "It just hasn't happened."

Awkward Conversation 5: **Someone You Don't Know Well Asks for a Recommendation**

> **Problem:** Your credibility and livelihood are at risk if you recommend someone whose capabilities and character you can't vouch for firsthand.
>
> **Desired outcome:** You only recommend people whose work you know.
>
> **Tactful response:** "I never recommend anyone unless I know his or her work. Why don't you send me a few samples of what you've done? Then I'll see what I can do."

Awkward Conversation 6: **A Colleague or Friend Wants Your Relationship to Take a Romantic Turn**

> **Problem:** A harsh rejection of a friend or coworker's romantic overtures can lead to hard feelings and an uncomfortable situation.
>
> **Desired outcome:** Maintain a good relationship.
>
> **Tactful response:** Be polite, friendly, but firm and direct. To your coworker you can say, "I have a rule that I never get romantically involved with people at work. So I'm sorry. The answer is no, but it was nice of you to ask." To dissuade a friend with romantic notions, you can say, "You're just a good friend and that's the way I want to keep it."

Awkward Conversation 7: **A Person Aggressively Challenges Your Opinion**

> **Problem:** A difference of opinion can quickly escalate into a full-blown argument.
>
> **Desired outcome:** Avoid a confrontation.

Tactful response: "We obviously have a different view of the situation. Let's agree to disagree." If he or she continues to challenge or needle you, calmly state, "Please, let's agree to disagree and leave it at that."

Awkward Conversation 8: You Say Something That Has Offended or Upset Someone

Problem: The harder you try to talk your way out of the indiscretion, the worse it gets.

Desired outcome: Get past the comment and change the topic.

Tactful response: Quickly apologize. Say, "Oh, I'm so sorry I said that! I don't know what I was thinking—I was thoughtless. Please forgive me."

Awkward Conversation 9: There Are Long Periods of Silence during a Conversation

Problem: Short periods of silence are a natural part of conversation, but if the silence goes on for too long, it will make people feel uncomfortable.

Desired outcome: Reignite the conversation after a long, uncomfortable silence.

Tactful response: "I was just thinking about something you said a few minutes ago," or "I just remembered something that I've been meaning to tell (ask) you."

Awkward Conversation 10: You Ask about a Spouse Recently Divorced or Deceased

Problem: Inadvertently bringing up painful personal experiences makes most people uncomfortable or can unleash a barrage of venom that you do not want to hear.

Desired outcome: Acknowledge the person's situation.

Tactful response: "I'm sorry to hear that. I didn't know. How are you doing otherwise?"

Awkward Conversation 11: A Person at a Party Does Nothing but Complain and Gossip

Problem: Negative conversations can darken the mood of partygoers.

Desired outcome: Change the topic to a more upbeat subject.

Tactful response: Say, "Well, that's a downer. I want to change the subject. Let me tell you about something good that happened to me recently." Or, to a gossip, you might say, "I don't talk about other people's problems, particularly if they are friends or colleagues. Let's talk about something more positive, like . . ."

Awkward Conversation 12: A Relative Is Pressuring You into Doing Something

Problem: Pressure or manipulation usually creates resentment.

Desired outcome: Say no without feeling guilty or causing a ruckus.

Tactful response: Don't make up excuses. Be direct and firm and calmly say, "No, I don't care to do that."

Awkward Conversation 13: Someone Offers You Unsolicited Advice

Problem: Although it may be well-meaning, unsolicited advice is annoying at best; if unrelenting, it can be condescending and manipulative.

Desired outcome: Show appreciation but discourage further suggestions.

Tactful response: Be cool and polite. Say, "I appreciate that you're trying to help, but I'll work it out on my own."

Awkward Conversation 14: A Friend Only Calls You to Whine or Ask for Favors

Problem: If you don't put a stop to a friend's constant complaining or seeking help, your friendship will suffer.

Desired outcome: Discourage complaining and encourage personal responsibility.

Tactful response: Gently say, "I don't know what to tell you other than you're going to have to work out these problems yourself. There must be something positive happening in your life, and I'd much rather hear about that."

Awkward Conversation 15: Asking for a Favor or Help

Problem: Hinting or implying that you need a favor rather than directly asking for help can leave a friend or colleague confused and even feeling manipulated.

Desired outcome: Get the help you need without manipulation.

Tactful response: Directly say, "I have a (big/little) favor to ask you. If you can't help me out, just say so and I'll understand."

Tactfully Handling Awkward Conversations Leads to Better Relationships

It's okay to assertively speak up for yourself in awkward conversations. After all, how else can you expect people to know what you want or don't want if you don't tell them? Sure, it takes some extra thought, pluck, and patience to assert yourself when dealing with a difficult coworker or pushy relative, but using *T-A-C-T*—Thinking before you speak; Actively listening; Considering the outcome; and Treading lightly—will create a better result and change the dynamics of your relationships. Your friends, colleagues, and family will start to relate to you in a different way. Yes, old communication habits die hard—especially between people who have known each other for a long time—but practice and a desire to improve your communication will create better personal and professional relationships.

8

Closing Conversations and Leaving a Great Impression

Help, I'm trapped in a conversation and I can't get out!
—Anonymous blog posting

All conversations must come to an end sometime. Since there's a natural flow to most conversations, there is a right time to bring conversations to a successful close.

The Best Time to End a Conversation

Whether you are engaged in a brief or lengthy conversation, be aware of the dynamics involved in ending conversations in a positive manner. If you wait too long, you and your partner will feel the strain and become uncomfortable, anxious, or even bored. The easiest moment to end the conversation has already passed. If you are anxious, especially during short periods of silence, you may end the conversation earlier than necessary, and in an abrupt manner. This will leave your partner with the impression that you don't feel comfortable about the conversation or him or her.

It's best to end a conversation after both parties have expressed themselves to each other and when the time seems right or demands that you go your separate ways. It's important to end conversations in a warm and engaging manner so that you'll both feel good about the exchange that has occurred.

Closing a Conversation in a Way That Leaves a Positive Impression

There are natural pauses between sentences and topics of discussion, and it's wise to wait for these opportune moments to bring your conversation to a close. When you feel the time is right to close the conversation—that is, the discussion has come to a conclusion or one of the parties has to leave—take an active role and begin to send signals that you are ready to leave. Briefly summarize the main ideas your partner has been expressing. This shows the other person that you were listening and that you understood, and it also signals a conclusion to the discussion.

End Your Conversations Tactfully

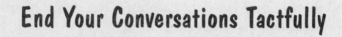

Step 1: Restate something interesting the other person said.

Step 2: Say you enjoyed the chat.

Step 3: (Optional) Say, "Let's talk again soon."

Step 4: Use the person's name and say good-bye.

If you are discussing a particular current event, and you want to send a conclusion signal, you could say, "It certainly sounds like you're well informed about the problem. I'll read that article you were talking about."

After you send a signal that you want to end a conversation, it's good to plan to see the other person again (only if you really want to) by setting a meeting for the future. Instead of closing with the customary cliché "Why don't we get together sometime?" (which usually means never), be more specific about an event such as a movie or dinner, and a time within the next week or so. In a friendly and direct way, you could say, for example, "John, I've enjoyed talking with you. How about getting together next week for dinner or a movie? I'll give you a call."

In this way, you express your interest in your partner while leaving an open invitation to meet again. This is particularly effective for developing friendships and relationships. Remember to use your partner's name when you say good-bye, and use open, friendly body language (eye contact, smiling, and a warm handshake). Then be on your way. Avoid long-drawn-out good-byes.

Getting Out of Problem Conversations

There are times when the nature of a conversation, or the person you're speaking with, makes you prefer to end the conversation and withdraw sooner than later but without offending the other person. For example, if you are cornered by a long-winded bore at a party who has been bragging about his exploits for some time, then try the following strategy to end the conversation.

Wait for a slight pause between words or sentences, and then quickly interject (an acceptable form of interruption) a few rapid yes/no or closed-ended questions, thus interrupting the bore's flow of words and giving you the conversational ball. (Remember, you can direct a conversation by asking questions.) Then restate in a few sentences an acknowledgment of your partner's last few statements, and get ready to make your getaway. You can say, "Well, it sounds like you enjoy your work! Good luck on your next project. I'm going to mosey along and say hello to a friend of mine," or "I'm going to get some hors d'oeuvres now, if you'll excuse me." After smiling, shaking hands, and using his name, say, "It was nice talking to you." Then move directly out of the situation.

You may be worrying, *But what if I don't know anyone else at the party! I can't just stand around! He'll see me standing there and become offended!* Try this simple solution: Go refill your glass, get something to eat, or visit the bathroom, then take a few moments to survey the situation. Look for the most open and receptive group or person in the room. Proceed there directly and engage in conversation. If you're really sharp, you can spot your likely person or group before you deliver your conversation closer.

FAQ

I hate it when I'm at a party and get trapped by a complainer. I know I need to be a good listener, but after a while I feel like I'm being used. How can I tactfully end a conversation with someone who complains too much?

Handling the Complainer

The complainer usually talks about personal problems, misfortune, sickness, and other unfortunate events. In most cases, people who focus on unpleasant topics are looking for sympathy. No one enjoys listening to the constant complainer. Therefore, after listening for free information and details of the problem, ask a few yes/no or closed-ended questions to break the flow of complaints and to allow you to direct the conversation to a conclusion.

Express some words of sympathy, such as "It sounds like you're having a tough time," or "I'm sorry to hear that you're having so much trouble." This will indicate to the other person that you have been listening and empathize with her problem.

When handling the complainer, it is perfectly acceptable to offer a few words of unsolicited advice or general words of wisdom and encouragement, such as: "Just hang in there—it'll work out," or "If it makes you feel any better, you're not the only one who is having that problem." Then, with sincere feeling, say, "I hope things work out for you," smile, give the person a warm hand-shake, and add, "I'm going to go say hello to a friend of mine." Then say good-bye, using the person's name, and move quickly out of the situation.

FAQ

My friend always dumps all his problems on me when he calls on the telephone. He moans that his girlfriend isn't around enough, that he's unappreciated on the job, and that his parents still treat him like a child. I know that good friends are supposed to be good listeners, but after a while I feel like I'm being used. How can I tactfully end the conversation?

It's gratifying to help a friend who has troubles, and yes, a good friend is a good listener. But there's a limit to how much complaining even a good friend can listen to. The key word here is *limit*. Limit how much time you devote to discussing a friend's problems and advice that you offer. No matter how much you might want to help, the truth is that no one can solve your friend's problems except him.

Limit the time you talk about his problems by first empathizing with his plight. This validates his feelings and shows you are listen-ing. Asking him to come up with some options clearly demon-strates that you're not going to be his problem solver. For example, you might say, "Sam, it sounds like you're going through a rough time at work right now. So, what are your options?" He may respond that he doesn't have a clue, with the hope that you will offer advice or continue discussing his problem. Instead, you can say, "Well, I'm sure you can come up with something."

Since friendship is a two-way street, you have the right to expect him to be a good listener too. Change the subject to something that you want to talk about by saying, "By the way, I've been meaning to tell you about . . ." Then end your conversation on a positive note by saying, "I hope things improve for you at work."

The Last Few Words

To summarize, when you end conversations:

- Always attempt to end the exchange on a friendly note. This lets the other participant feel good about the exchange.
- Use the other person's name, add a compliment such as "It's been great talking with you," and then say good-bye with a handshake.
- Attempt to meet the person again for a specific activity at a time not too far into the future—say, a week or so. Say: "I'm looking forward to seeing you again."
- Tell your partner you enjoyed the conversation and you are going to mosey on to chat with someone else, get a drink, say hello to a friend, or whatever you wish to do, and then do it.
- Keep your good-bye short and sweet and, most of all, warm and friendly.

Part III

Navigating Online Networks to
Expand Your Business, Social, and
Personal Relationships

9

Exploring Social Networks
and Blogs

The Internet is the most important single development in the
history of human communication since the invention of call
waiting.
> —Dave Barry (1947–), author, columnist

I got a surprising Facebook message not long ago. "Are you the
Mr. Gabor who taught at Bradshaw Elementary school in the late
1970s? If so, I was one of your 5th grade students!" Wow! Talk
about how a social network like Facebook helps people reconnect—and after more than thirty years! But what happened next
was even more amazing. Within two weeks after I sent my past
student a note saying how thrilled I was to hear from him and
accept his request to be a Facebook "friend," another six students
from that class sent me Facebook messages. Now, thanks to Facebook, we are all friends and reconnected online!

Before the birth of Facebook, LinkedIn, and other social networks, people met and talked with one another where they lived,
worked, played, worshipped, and traveled. Of course, most people
still chat face-to-face, but as social networking websites have in-
creased in popularity, these virtual meeting places have become
convenient ways for people to socialize, connect, and establish
friendships. Since many social networking sites are free and international, it's no wonder that millions of people around the world
chat and become friends online.

Joining social networks is easy, but because this modern way of socializing is evolving and expanding at such a rapid rate, it can be a challenge, too. It is useful to know how to find websites, blogs, and people who share your interests. Once you have connected, you can let others know who you are and engage in online conversations using proper "friending" etiquette and following practical security guidelines. There are several kinds of social networking sites that cater to different groups, ages, interests, and goals. Among the most popular are Facebook, MySpace, LinkedIn, Twitter, eHarmony.com, and Match.com.

Get Started with Facebook and MySpace

Facebook and MySpace are the most widely used social networking websites for meeting people, making new friends, reconnecting with old friends, and engaging people in conversation. These websites are designed to help members who may or may not live in the same area to chat, get to know one another, and share experiences and other areas of interest. You can join discussions or share news or information through posts on members' walls. A wall is a space on each user's profile page that allows friends to post messages for the user to see and displays the time and date the message was written. You can also chat with members directly via e-mail. Although Facebook and MySpace were originally oriented toward online socializing, today many small businesses, corporations, nonprofit organizations, and professional service providers also use these social networks to market their products and services to millions of their friends or members. You can talk about just about anything on Facebook, but the most popular topics include celebrities, movies, sports, music, business, and technology.

One reason for the immense popularity of Facebook and MySpace is that they are free to join. Plus, it's easy to expand your network of friends and connect with other members who share your interests, experiences, and goals. With a few clicks of the mouse you can connect or reconnect with people you know from work, high school, or college, and/or members of organizations to which you currently or once belonged. Not only can you find old friends who you haven't talked to for years, you can make many new friends too!

After signing up for a Facebook or MySpace account and creating a profile, joining conversations is easy. You can:

- Look for people you know and send them an e-mail and invitation to be your friend
- Follow the comments of your online friends
- Post some comments and questions of your own
- Answer questions and post comments to your online friends
- Share links and news related to industry-, social-issue-, or community-related events
- Connect with other members through discussions and groups

Make Professional Contacts on LinkedIn

Do you want to network with your peers without leaving your office? Are you looking for job opportunities in your area of expertise? Do you want to market to professionals who might be interested in your services or products? Would you like background information about prospects before you meet them on a sales call? These are just a few of the many benefits you'll find when you join LinkedIn, a free business-oriented social network where you can read member profiles and join online group discussions and communities of professionals based on common interests, experience, affiliation, and goals. And, like most other social networks, it's free and simple to use. LinkedIn claims to have fifty million members worldwide, with thousands of professional groups where you can connect, chat, and stay in touch with your peers, industry experts, coworkers, colleagues, customers, and vendors.

On LinkedIn, consider joining online conversations in corporate and college alumni groups, nonprofit organizations, trade groups, conferences, and industry-specific groups. Business development, media and news, business, and technology are just a few of the categories of discussion groups that provide an interactive and professional forum where you can talk about issues relevant to the members of the group. For example, members share industry news, make announcements, post and explore job opportunities, and network prior to events. Most professionals agree that if they first converse online via LinkedIn, it's easier to break the ice when they meet in person.

When you find a group that interests you, click on the group manager and look over his or her profile. If you have any questions about the group, you can send the group manager a message. Then, if you think that the group may be a good match for you, click on the "Join Group" link to request to join the group. Keep in mind that the group manager reviews all requests to join the group and that to join a corporate or college group you may be required to have a valid e-mail account.

After signing up for a LinkedIn account and creating a profile, it is easy to initiate conversations with other members:

- Look for people you know on LinkedIn and send them an email
- If you know them and they know you, send an invitation to be a contact
- Look for professional groups that you can join
- Answer questions of other users
- Write recommendations for your contacts
- Ask happy clients on LinkedIn to write recommendations for you
- Share links and news related to industry-related events
- Connect with other members through discussions and groups

Twitter Shares "What Are You Doing Now?" with Anyone Who Is Interested

Twitter is a service started in 2006 where users post and read 140-character messages known as "tweets" that answer this question: "What are you doing now?" Tweets are displayed on the author's profile page and delivered to the author's subscribers, who are known as "followers." As in other social networks, people write about popular topics such as food, politics, travel, and even celebrities' every movement and thought. According to Twitter expert Joel Comm, "There might be several million people on the site talking about what they are doing and chatting with other Twitterers, but you really do feel that every one of them could be your friend if you wanted them to be."

After signing up for a Twitter account and creating a profile, joining conversations on Twitter is easy. Simply:

- Post questions and answer tweets daily to spark discussion or evoke a response.
- Follow the tweets of others and respond in a timely manner.
- Share links and news related to industry-, social-issue-, or community-related events.
- Connect with other Twitterers through other social networks and on discussion forums.

Connecting with the One You Love through Dating Websites

Are you sick of getting chatted up in bars? Have you had it with going out on blind dates? Do you get tongue-tied at singles and speed-dating events? If you are looking for an alternative to these and other traditional ways to meet and find a mate, why not join the millions of singles who have flocked to popular dating websites like eHarmony.com and Match.com to find a compatible partner. Although fees and matchmaking methods of online dating websites vary, most begin by having members complete a detailed relationship-oriented questionnaire. Next, members receive possible candidates for dates. Members of eHarmony.com, for example, are presented with "a pool of matches scientifically evaluated to be compatible with them." Match.com claims to provide a "variety of powerful search tools to help you find people based on their interests, background, age, location, and more." The next step in this modern dating ritual is an opportunity to get to know their matches online without revealing their identity. Then, if both people are comfortable, they can reveal their identities, communicate directly, and, if they agree, meet in person.

Online dating social networks have at least three advantages over other methods of meeting the love of your life. First, they promise to connect you with a certain number of promising dates who have been selected for you based on sophisticated couple-matching software, supposedly eliminating obvious mismatches. Second, the online dating websites allow people to share their interests, see photos, and read personal profiles so they can easily chat and get to know one another over time without having to meet in person. This relieves the anxiety many people feel about going on blind dates or meeting at singles events or in bars. Finally, if the people are interested in meeting, they can set up a real date. If not, an online rejection on a dating website isn't nearly as personal as it is face-to-face or on the telephone.

Niche Social Networks Are Fun to Explore

Big social networks have the greatest number of members, but you will find it enlightening and entertaining to browse and engage in conversation on some of the small niche websites with forums and blogs too. Go to www.wikipedia.com and type "social networking websites" in the search window. In seconds you'll find the names of more than two hundred social networking websites with brief descriptions, number of registered users, global page ranking, and registration requirements. It's truly amazing to see the vast number of social networks that cater to every conceivable hobby or interest, and most of their members love to chat and are open to making online friends.

Blogs Are Another Great Way to Engage in Online Conversations

I recently learned firsthand how commenting on a blog posting can lead to a profitable business relationship. I had read a blog posting on a social network for database managers that urged techies to get out from behind their computers to network with their peers. I was happy to see an IT (information technology) professional espousing the benefits of networking, but I was even more excited when I saw that he had mentioned my book *How to Start a Conversation and Make Friends*.

To show my appreciation, I sent the blogger a brief e-mail thanking him for recommending my book to his peers. In addition, I posted a response to a question he had about remembering names in the comment section on his blog. Over the next few days we exchanged several comments, e-mails, and telephone conversations. Within a few weeks of our first online chat, he hired me as a networking coach, recommended me on LinkedIn, and hired me as a speaker for his association's annual meeting!

Today, millions of individuals, businesses, and organizations around the world have blogs to provide online readers with commentary, news, views on particular subjects, or personal online diaries. According to social networking researchers, blogs are incredibly popular because readers can interact with the bloggers and other readers by posting comments—and it's free and easy to get started. To find a vast number of blogs where people discuss every topic under the sun, visit the popular blog search engine website technorati.com or blogsearch.google.com. There you'll find listings for blogs on subjects ranging from anime to zoology and everything in between. Then it's up to you to log on and engage the blogger and his or her followers in a conversation.

FAQ

I'm overwhelmed by all the blogs. Which do you recommend visiting?

Here Are a Few Popular Blogs and Their Topics

There are literally millions of blogs and websites, but here are six that are among the most popular according to Technorati and Wikipedia.

- **Huffingtonpost.com** offers coverage of politics, media, business, entertainment, living, style, the green movement, world news, and comedy with a liberal slant and is a top destination for news, blogs, and original content.
- **Techcrunch.com** profiles start-up companies, technology products, and websites.
- **Mashable.com** offers news about YouTube, Facebook, Google, Twitter, MySpace, Apple, and start-ups, but it also reports on less well-known social networking and social media sites.
- **Gawker.com** boasts that it is "the source for daily Manhattan media news and gossip" and focuses on celebrities and the media industry.
- **Boingboing.net** is a group blog that focuses on cultural curiosities and interesting technologies.
- **Thedailybeast.com** reports U.S. news and opinions. About one-third of its content is original, while the rest is aggregated links to articles written by other news outlets.

Explore Many Social Networks and Blogs—Participate in a Few

Whether you explore social networks for social reasons or business, it's a good idea to visit the popular sites before signing up as a member to see what they have to offer, their rules, whom they cater to, and if there are any membership fees. After you have all the information, then you can decide on which ones to join. Don't worry if you feel a bit overwhelmed by the sheer number of social networks and blogs that you find online. It's impossible to join every conversation on the social networks you visit or to write meaningful comments on every blog you read. That's why experts suggest that at first you join one or two social networks and comment on just a few blogs. The key is to participate on a regular basis.

Many blogs may not require much more than your e-mail and username for you to post a comment. However, to get started on social networks, you'll need to take one more important step after you sign up to become a member. You'll be asked to create an online profile that tells others who you are, what you like to talk about, and—most important—that you are open to contact and making new friends. A good online profile breaks the ice for you before the conversation even starts.

10

Creating a Winning Online Profile

I was looking in the mirror the other day and I realized I haven't
changed much since I was in my twenties. The only difference is
I look a whole lot older now.
  —George Carlin (1937–2008), American comedian and author

Wouldn't it be great if you knew what others online liked to talk
about—their preferences, profession, education, and even some
background information—before you exchanged a single word?
You can—if you check out their online profiles! And that's easy,
because most social media websites like Facebook, MySpace,
LinkedIn, and Twitter ask people to complete profiles that include
a username, some basic information, details about what you are
looking for (a job, friends, mate, business contacts, etc.), "About
Me" and "Favorites" sections, and a photo.

Your Online Profile Speaks Before You Do

Some people stretch the truth in their online profiles, and that can
lead to miscommunication and credibility problems. For example,
I had a client whose profile on a dating website stated he was
forty-three, when actually he was over fifty. Under "Education" he
wrote *Master's* but, in fact, he only had a bachelor's degree. He was
several inches shorter than he stated in his profile, and his picture
was about ten years out of date, showing him ten pounds lighter
and with considerably more hair. When I asked him why he did
this and pointed out the obvious problems he would face on a first
date, he responded, "Everyone stretches the truth on their profiles,

and if I don't, no one will contact me. Anyway, I can come clean if and when we meet." All I could say was "Good luck!"

Since all relationships—both online and in person—are based on trust, a less-than-candid profile will hardly start the relationship on the right foot and can cause some embarrassing conversations. Therefore, the most important profile strategy is: Be yourself. Twitter expert Joel Comm recommends in his excellent book *Twitter Power* that you think carefully about and then create an inviting and accurate profile before sending your first message. Other social media experts agree that a friendly, useful, eye-catching, and honest profile is the foundation of good online communication. Your profile plays an important role in engaging in meaningful conversation, attracting others, getting accepted into online communities, and fostering online relationships.

A well-thought-out and interesting profile that reveals topics you are passionate about (your "hot buttons") helps you and your online friends get to know one another faster, and enables you to have more fun in the process. Snappy profiles help people to quickly and easily find out loads of information about one another so that when they chat online or face-to-face, keeping the conversation popping with energy and interest won't be a problem.

Six Tips for Creating a Winning Online Profile

Your profile creates your online image and gives others clues about your interests and what you like to talk about. Here are six tips to create a friendly, receptive, and straightforward image while providing the right kinds of "free information" that will encourage others to contact you and initiate online conversations.

Tip #1: Be Conversational, Specific, and Interested in Others

When we meet face-to-face, we smile, make eye contact, and chat informally as we get to know one another. This usually gets the best results, because informal conversation tends to put people at ease. Your online profile can be informal, too, if it reads more like a conversation than a bio on a job résumé. Being conversational in your online profile will give people a sense of your personality and that you are friendly. It will create interest in you and demonstrate your interest in others. Add specific yet brief and colorful descriptions to the facts about your background, experiences, and preferences to provide interesting details that people can ask you about. Plus, adding your desire to connect with others who share your social, professional, and, if applicable, personal goals will make you appear more conversational, approachable, and interesting.

Here's an example: "I'm a food-loving baby boomer happily married and living in New York City since 1979. When I'm not writing self-help books like *How to Start a Conversation and Make Friends* or teaching conversation workshops, I'm playing folk and rock guitar, listening to jazz and blues, gardening (my nickname is Donnie Flowers), traveling, and exploring restaurants with my wife and friends. I love talking to people anywhere and everywhere—including online—and finding out what we have in common." These are the kinds of details to include on your Facebook and MySpace profiles.

Tip #2: Modify Your Profiles for Different Social Media Websites

Twitter expert and author Joel Comm recommends opening multiple accounts with different profiles so that you can write about different subjects. Extend that idea to all social networks and you'll see that customizing your bio to fit different websites will help you reach the people with whom you'd most like to meet and connect.

For example, if you are an accountant whose hobby is renovating old boats, your business-oriented Twitter profile might say, "I just published a book of business advice that I've given my clients over the last forty years." Your second Twitter account profile might say, "My hobby is turning old boats into beautiful little ships."

Emphasize fun activities you like to do with friends in your profiles on Facebook and MySpace. For example, "I enjoy playing team sports like volleyball, softball, and bowling. I also like to go to movies and foreign films with friends and then talk about them over a coffee, a drink, or a meal."

For profiles on dating websites, add some lifestyle goals and what you want to share with a potential partner in addition to your interests, background, and current activities. For example, "To me it's really important that I share with my partner not only what we like to do for fun and matters related to politics, money, and religion, but also how we deal with day-to-day issues."

Write more formal profiles for business websites like LinkedIn that focus on your professional experience, your goals, and the networking activities you do with colleagues to further your career. For example, "For the past . . . years, I've happily worked for . . . as a . . . helping clients such as . . . My immediate professional goals are to . . ."

Tip #3: Be Discriminating about Your Self-Disclosures

People typically check profiles on multiple sites to get a broader view of someone whom they want to contact. Therefore, depending on the website, it is useful to include some personal information in your profile, but don't go too far with personal revelations. It's best to be judicious about your self-disclosures and omit anything specific about your health, finances, or other personal background that might compromise your privacy, might adversely affect a present relationship, or could be used in some other unintended way. "When in doubt, leave it out" is a good rule to follow if you are not sure whether to include or omit some fact about yourself from your profile.

However, you can also write your disclosures in a nonspecific way. For example, regarding your health, you can say, "I feel young for a person my age." Regarding your finances, you can say, "I've been happily employed for . . . years." Regarding a past relationship, you can say, "I agree with the old saying ''Tis better to have loved and lost, than never to have loved at all.'"

Tip #4: Pepper Your Profile with Your Hot Buttons

Are you so passionate about food that you take cooking classes, visit many restaurants, and experiment with new ingredients and recipes? Do you volunteer for a local hospital or animal shelter? Can you fix just about anything that has a motor or modem? Are you preparing a vacation around your state, country, or globe? Have you built a business from the ground up? Highlighting your passions, meaningful experiences, and talents in your profile gives others a window into what makes you unique and offers them plenty of topics that they know you are ready, willing, and able to talk about. For example, you can write, "I'm so passionate about . . . that I wake up every morning thinking about . . ."

Tip #5: Use a Recent Photo That Shows Your Eyes and Smile

In face-to-face conversations, people look for eye contact and a smile as signs of approachability and openness. A close-up photo of you with a gentle smile looking directly at the camera serves the same purpose for your online profile. It says you are friendly, trustworthy, and willing to communicate. Outdated photos, pictures in which you look considerably different (longer hair, big weight changes, etc.), or ones in which your face is too small, can mislead and create this potentially embarrassing comment when you meet in person: "You don't look anything like your photo." Consider getting a professional head shot for a profile on LinkedIn or other career-oriented websites.

FAQ

I want to be judged based on who I am, not what I look like in a photograph. Is there anything wrong with that?

Some people choose not to include a photo in their profile because they don't want to be prejudged. Instead, they may use an avatar, a cartoon character, or a generic silhouette in their profile. However, omitting a photo from your profile may send other messages, including a lack of self-confidence about your appearance or that the facts in the profile do not match the photo. Most people don't look like models, so don't worry if your photo isn't perfect. Potential friends just want to know what you look like, so do your best to find a photo where your smile and eyes say: "I'm friendly and willing to talk to you."

Tip #6: Use Photos That Tell a Short Story about You

Photos showing what we look like and what we like to do help us make decisions and form opinions about one another. For example, a photo that shows a man at an animal shelter caring for dogs or cats shows that he loves animals and wants to help find them homes. A photo of a woman on a bicycle or hiking in the countryside shows that she likes to exercise outside in beautiful places and cares about her fitness and health. The more photos in your profile that tell positive stories about you, the more likely people are to find you interesting and appealing. While some websites like LinkedIn use only one photo, Facebook and other websites allow several photos. Whichever site you are on, choose the photo or photos that will best project the image you want.

Make Your Online Profile Snap, Crackle, and Pop with Personality

The more meaningful and colorful details you put into your profile, the easier it will be for others to get a sense of your personality as well as interests, experiences, and goals you may have in common—and all before you've exchanged one word! So, now that you know how to create your profile on your favorite social media websites, the next step is to join the online conversations.

11

Joining Online Conversations and Making Contacts

> I got a lot of best friends. Some o' them I don't even hardly know!
> —Archie Bunker, character from television series *All in the Family*
> played by Carroll O'Connor (1924–2001), American actor,
> producer, and director

There are many ways to join online conversations on social networking sites, blogs, and Twitter, but not all lead to productive exchanges. For example, after several people posted unflattering comments on a popular website devoted to books about a bestselling author's latest novel, she responded with a long and equally nasty online post. Network members quickly answered with even more scathing feedback of her work. On another social network dedicated to sci-fi themes, passionate debates between fans of *Star Trek* and *Star Wars* quickly spiraled out of control into vindictive exchanges. Then there are the devoted users of Macs and PCs who got so involved in heated technical discussions that they ended up insulting each other in their postings on a professional user group website. None of these examples bodes well for developing future relationships.

Set a Friendly Tone to Your Online Conversations

How you engage other social network members in conversation sets the tone for all the interactions that follow—both online and in person. By tactfully joining conversations and following the basic and generally accepted rules of online etiquette, not only will you make a positive first impression, but you'll have a better chance of creating online relationships that will grow and flourish. Rather than approaching online conversations as confrontations, look at them as opportunities to connect, interact, and make new friends.

Four Steps to Joining Online Conversations

While there are many ways to join online conversations, the following four steps will facilitate the process.

Step #1: Observe Before You Comment

Follow an online discussion for a while before posting a comment. This will give you a feeling for the group culture, values, and conversation styles of the people on the site. Match your conversation style to the formality or informality of the online community.

Step #2: Break the Ice with a Short Positive Comment or Easy-to-Answer Question

The easiest way to join an online conversation is with a positive comment. It's okay to post comments like "Excellent post," "Ditto," or "Rock on," but don't stop there. Follow up with a short and upbeat comment or easy-to-answer question. This will help you come across as friendly and genuine and show that you want to join the conversation.

Write your comments in upper- and lowercase letters, like any typical written correspondence. Avoid using ALL CAPS because it means YOU'RE SHOUTING. For example, if someone wrote, YOU DID WHAT? in an online conversation, not only would it be considered rude, it would show that the sender did not know this basic online rule of etiquette.

Step #3: Get More Involved by Offering Comments That Have Value and Encourage a Response

To get involved in the conversation and stimulate the discussion:

- **Ask an open-ended question:** "What is it about . . . that you found so . . . ?"
- **Share your perspective with a comment:** "I also had a funny experience when I . . ."
- **Elaborate on a point:** "To add another example to your point about . . ."

Offer your experience or insights that inform or help others. Avoid long, rambling posts or comments that stray from the topic. Instead, include in your posts questions and requests for ideas and suggestions. For example, "I understand your dilemma firsthand. I had a similar situation. Here's how I handled it . . ." or "Interesting problem. What are your options?"

Avoid Sarcastic Remarks and Restrain Dissenting Opinions or Complaints

Are your comments friendly and thought-provoking or sarcastic and opinionated? Your comments communicate more than your knowledge or experience. They give others a sense of your personality and attitude concerning the ideas of others. Social networks are forums for discussion, so you can offer dissenting views. However, harsh or highly opinionated comments will likely alienate others on the site and leave them with a negative impression of you. If you disagree with someone's post, post a few questions to show that you want to understand the views and opinions of others before posting strongly worded dissenting views. Carefully word and review your dissenting opinion to be sure it doesn't sound argumentative or condescending. Never use blogs or social networking websites to bad-mouth someone or besmirch that person's reputation or air your personal grievances with individuals or organizations. Here are a few other dos and don'ts:

- **Do** review all the messages on a topic before you write a response to avoid reacting to a comment out of context.
- **Don't** take an opposing view for the sake of argument.
- **Do** ignore any statements by others designed to inflame or incite.
- **Don't** try to make yourself look smart by pointing out the mistakes of others.
- **Do** comment on something you can agree with before offering a dissenting view.
- **Don't** present your opinions as facts or the only possible way of looking at an issue.
- **Do** present your views with the caveats "From my perspective . . ." or "It's been my experience . . ."

Step #4: Comment Regularly and Quickly

If you want to become involved in online conversations and build a bond with others online, then submit your comments in a timely manner and on a regular basis. You don't need to comment on everything—just what you find interesting or useful.

Invitation Etiquette for Social Networks: You Don't Get a Second Chance to Make a Good First Impression

Most social networks make it easy for members to join one another's network of contacts or friends. However, you have the right to decline requests to join your network from people you don't know or who are not recommended by someone you know and trust. Experts recommend that you establish an "I need to know you first" criterion for accepting requests to be a "friend" or "contact." While you should promptly reply to a contact who took the time to write you a personal note to connect, do avoid just clicking

"Accept" without, at the very least, checking the person's home page, profile, and other friends. When a stranger sends you an invitation to join your network or "add request," you can:

- Ask, "Have we met?" or respond, "Please remind me how I know you"
- Ignore or reject the invite if you don't know the person
- Be polite if you choose to reject a stranger's request to add you as a friend, contact, or connection. You can respond, "Thank you for your invitation, but I don't accept 'add' requests from people I don't know."

Eliminate "Do I Know You?" Responses and Decrease Rejections
- Include a brief note when you offer an invitation to be part of your network. Explain how you know the person.
- Ask a mutual online friend or contact to introduce you
- If you want to contact a long-lost friend, send an e-mail to say hello before you send a request to add him or her as a friend or contact.
- Exchange a few e-mails before sending an invitation to join your network or a request to join his or her network
- Use the features on Facebook and LinkedIn that allow you to "suggest a friend" or "introduce a friend" through a mutual contact

FAQ _____
Are there really rules of online etiquette?
_____

There are rules of etiquette for online conversations. If you want to make friends and not alienate other members of online communities, then make sure you don't make the following mistakes. However, if you do, be sure to correct them.

10 Biggest Conversation Mistakes People Make Online and How to Correct Them

Mistake #1: Relentlessly e-mailing your social networking contacts with pitches for your products or services.

Correction: Send articles, links, and other information that your contacts or friends will find useful.

Mistake #2: Sending your online contacts unsolicited political, religious, or sexually oriented matter.

Correction: Like face-to-face conversations, it's best to keep sex, politics, and religion out of your online conversations.

Mistake #3: Asking for endorsements, referrals, or help from individuals you don't know.

Correction: First, build your relationship by working together on a project. Then ask for an endorsement, referral, or help.

Mistake #4: Ignoring or losing touch with your old contacts.

Correction: Send short, personal "We've been out of touch for a while. How are you?" notes to contacts who you haven't recently heard from.

Mistake #5: Prematurely recommending new online friends to your established contacts.

Correction: Make it a policy to have several conversations with new online friends before you offer them a referral.

Mistake #6: Posting sloppily written comments.

Correction: Reread and check your comments *before* clicking "Send" to make sure the information (dates, names, addresses, etc.) is correct.

Mistake #7: Turning differences of opinion into a flaming "war of words."

Correction: Offer a dissenting view without negating another's opinion. You can say, "I respect your views on this, but I see the situation (problem, solution, etc.) differently."

Mistake #8: Posting "candid" photos of yourself or friends.

Correction: Don't—even if you think your friends won't mind.

Mistake #9: Confronting someone who chooses not to accept your request to become a "friend" or "contact."

Correction: Accept the rejection and move on. The next time you send an invitation or request to join a network, include a personal note or introduction from a mutual contact.

Mistake #10: Trying to impress others by collecting hundreds of contacts and friends.

Correction: Focus on the quality, not quantity, of your contacts.

It's No Wonder So Many People Spend So Much Time Talking Online!

With all the opportunities afforded by online social networks and blogs, you'll never run out of things to say or people to talk to. You now know that it's important to know the basic "rules of the online road" so that you make a good first impression. But meeting new people on social networks is just the first step on the path to building face-to-face relationships.

12

Turning Online Conversations into Face-to-face Relationships

At every party there are two kinds of people—those who want to go home and those who don't. The trouble is, they are usually married to each other.
—Ann Landers (1918–2002), American advice columnist

In 2001, after reading the book *Bowling Alone* by Harvard sociologist Robert Putnam about how people don't know their neighbors anymore, three computer guys—Scott Heiferman, Matt Meeker, and Peter Kamali—had an idea. Heiferman said, "The Internet does a number of wonderful things, but it treats geography as irrelevant. We still live in a world where the local level is extremely important." And that's how Meetup.com—an easy-to-use website that helps people all around the world to organize local meetings—was born.

While the Internet is a great place to explore topics and chat online with people around the world, websites like Meetup.com and Tumblr.com allow members to find groups, join them, and meet people who share common interests, such as politics, books, games, movies, health, pets, careers, and hobbies, face-to-face.

To use one of these websites, simply enter your zip code or city and the topic you want to meet about. The Meetup website gives you places and times the group is scheduled to meet, plus the number of people who plan to attend. If a Meetup group for a particular topic doesn't exist in your community, you can start one. For example, Meetup.com helps you choose a theme, find the right members, and plan and schedule your first Meetup. Tumblr.

com offers Meetups and will even send you a free Meetup kit, complete with buttons, stickers, and nametags.

Meetups—from Online to Face Time

Thousands of groups get together in their communities each day using Meetup.com or any number of other social networking websites. Some meet for business, some meet for pleasure. Some meet for serious debate, others meet for serious fun. But one common goal meetup groups share is to make face-to-face connections and, hopefully, to start in-person relationships. Here are some of the popular general Meetup categories: Arts & Entertainment; Business & Career; Communities & Lifestyles; Cultures & Languages; Education; Health & Support; Hobbies; Internet & Technology; Parenting & Family; Pets & Animals; Politics & Activism; Religion & Beliefs; Science; Social; Sports & Recreation.

Break the Ice at Meetups Based on a Common Topic

Now that you're at a Meetup function, what do you say? The easiest way to break the ice at a Meetup group is to focus on the situation that brought you together and ask an easy-to-answer question; or make a short statement about yourself or something you like; or offer someone a sincere compliment and follow it with a question.

Here are some icebreakers and follow-up comments that show you are interested in continuing the conversation:

- **Business networking Meetup:** "What made you decide to go into business for yourself?"
- **Dancing Meetup:** "I love swing and tangos. What are your favorite dances?"
- **Dining Meetup:** "This is my first restaurant Meetup. What was the last place you dined at like?"
- **Executives in career transition Meetup:** "I'm looking at a new career in . . . What are you looking to do?"

- **Fashion Meetup:** "I love your outfit! Where did you find it?"
- **Gardening Meetup:** "I've planted five varieties of tomatoes. What are you growing this season?"
- **Hiking Meetup:** "I'm new in town and want to explore some of the parks and recreation areas. Can you recommend some good places to go in the area?"
- **Movie Meetup:** "A few of us go to a coffee shop after the movie to compare notes. You're welcome to join us."
- **Technology Meetup:** "I also belong to another Meetup group that meets to test and review new software. Have you ever tested new products?"
- **Wine-tasting Meetup:** "I hope the wines we taste tonight are as good as the ones at our last Meetup. Which ones did you like best?"

Tips for Continuing Conversations in Meetup Groups

- Listen for key words and free information to know what follow-up questions to ask and information to share.
- Ask open-ended questions and share information based on what others say and what you want to talk about.
- Gradually reveal information that allows others in the group to get to know you.
- Balance the amount you talk and listen.
- Never try to dominate the conversation or sell anyone anything.

FAQ

I've had several online conversations with someone on a popular social networking website. We've agreed to meet in person, but I'm not sure where or under what circumstances. Any suggestions?

A Note of Caution When Meeting in Person

Let's face it, even though most of the people you find in Meetup groups are honest and safe to be with, it is wise to follow some commonsense rules so you don't put yourself in a vulnerable or unsafe situation.

- Never give out your home address or financial or personal information to some you do not know well.

- If someone's behavior at the Meetup makes you feel uncomfortable, politely end the exchange and go talk to someone else. If the person harasses or threatens you, makes inappropriate requests, or uses sexually explicit language, be sure to report it to the webmaster of the website or to the group administrator.

- If you do decide to meet someone from the group in another setting, always choose a public place and, preferably, go there with other friends.

- If you are meeting the person for a "date," be sure to let someone else know when and where and with whom.

Turn Meetup Contacts into New Friends

One benefit of making contacts through Meetups is that you can decide if you want to develop a friendship with an individual outside the group's activities. For example, while attending a few Meetups of a local business group, I had several longer conversations with one member. As it turned out, we had several other common interests in addition to business. He is an ex–professional chef, and I have clients in the restaurant business. He traveled extensively in Asia, and I am fascinated with Japan and Japanese cuisine. He makes a great homemade salsa, and I grow tomatoes.

Since we had plenty to talk about, we agreed to meet on our own the following week for coffee at a local bakery. After chatting about food, travel, and the restaurant business, he offered to cook up a batch of his special salsa from my next crop of tomatoes. That sounded good to me!

This is how new friendships start as a result of an original online contact. If online relationships, like face-to-face friendships, are nurtured, they can continue to grow for years to come.

Part IV

*Boosting Your Conversations
to the Next Level*

13

Networking for Connections That Count

Don't worry about people stealing your ideas. If your ideas are
any good, you'll have to ram them down people's throats.
—Howard Aiken (1900–1973), inventor and early computer pioneer

Networking—you know it's important for your career and social
life, but if you're like a lot of people, you're not getting the results
you want from the time, effort, and money you spend attending
business and social events. First, take a short quiz to see how effectively you network now. Then follow the T-A-R-G-E-T and three
follow-up strategies to get better results from networking.

How Good of a Networker Are You?

Quiz Instructions

- *Honestly* answer how you actually network, not how you
  think you should network.
- Keep score: Often = 10 points; Sometimes = 5 points;
  Rarely or never = 0 point.
- Add up your points to get your score and find your
  networking level.

1. Do you attend networking events sponsored by more
   than one organization?

   Often ____   Sometimes ____   Rarely or never ____

2. Do you research the organization and attendees before the event?

   Often ____   Sometimes ____   Rarely or never ____

3. Do you identify people you want to talk to before you get to the event?

   Often ____   Sometimes ____   Rarely or never ____

4. At the event, do you find out the networking goals of others before sharing your networking goals?

   Often ____   Sometimes ____   Rarely or never ____

5. Do you join clusters of people who are already talking and networking?

   Often ____   Sometimes ____   Rarely or never ____

6. Do you describe the benefits of what you do or how you can help others?

   Often ____   Sometimes ____   Rarely or never ____

7. Do you limit your conversations based on the amount of time you spend at an event?

   Often ____   Sometimes ____   Rarely or never ____

8. Do you network with the "movers and shakers" at the events you attend?

   Often ____   Sometimes ____   Rarely or never ____

9. Do you suggest a follow-up e-mail, telephone, or meeting in person with people you chat with at events?

   Often ____   Sometimes ____   Rarely or never ____

10. After the event do you follow up in more than one way with people you met?

Often ____   Sometimes ____   Rarely or never ____

Your Score and Level

100–90 points: You are an **OUTSTANDING** networker. To widen your circle of influence beyond individual contacts, connect groups of people with intersecting business and social interests.

75–85 points: You are an **EXCELLENT** networker. To meet more targeted influencers and increase the quality of your networking contacts, seek introductions from your business and social associates.

55–70 points: You are a **PASSABLE** networker. To make networking pay off, turn targeted contacts into productive business or social relationships.

50 points and below: You are a **RETICENT** networker. To increase your business and social opportunities, reconnect with existing contacts and make a commitment to attend one or more business and social events a month.

Six T-A-R-G-E-T Strategies for Making Connections That Count

With so many networking opportunities at a meeting, party, or event and a limited time to chat, what can you do? Do what networking pros do: *T-A-R-G-E-T*, or prioritize, the people you want to talk to. You can do this before, during, and after the event by following these six strategies.

T in the Word T-A-R-G-E-T = Talk with People Who Have Influence and Power

To get the best networking results, you need to talk to those people who can help you make powerful connections. To accomplish this goal, spend most of your time at events networking with people who have the influence and power to connect you with others. Who are these people? If the event is sponsored by a business or organization, look at the website and event program for the names of:

- Officers and committee members
- Keynote speakers and workshop leaders
- Fund-raisers and publicity people
- Award recipients.

A in the Word T-A-R-G-E-T = Ask for a Guest List

This is one of my favorite and most useful networking tools. Why is a guest list so useful? Knowing who is attending an event gives you a powerful networking edge for the following reasons. You can:

- Identify and prioritize the people you most want to meet and talk to
- Find out background information or topics of interest to particular individuals
- Find out who the key people in the organization are
- Review the list of attendees to help you remember their names.

How can you get a guest list? Easy, just ask the host or event organizer the following:

I'm wondering, can I get the list of attendees for next week's event (party, workshop, meeting, etc.)? Knowing who is attending helps me network and remember people's names. I promise I won't use the list for marketing or anything else.

While some event planners will decline your request, most will agree if you reiterate that it is for your personal use and nothing more.

R *in the Word* T-A-R-G-E-T = Request an Introduction

As my mother often told me, "It's not just what you know—it's who you know." But what is more important when it comes to networking is: "Who knows you?" That's where requesting introductions can really help accelerate your networking success faster than almost anything else. When one person of influence introduces you to another person of influence, it sends a message that you are:

- important and worth knowing
- competent and professional
- reliable and trustworthy.

However, many influential people are reluctant to provide introductions or vouch for people they don't know well or for those whose business philosophies they do not support. Therefore, to minimize the chances of having your introduction request denied, make sure you:

- know the person you are asking to introduce you and make sure that he or she knows you
- explain the reasons why you want to be introduced to a particular individual
- are in good standing in your industry and organization
- do not hound the introducer or become aggressive if you do not get an immediate response.

G *in the Word* T-A-R-G-E-T = Give *Before You Receive*

"What you give out, you get back (although it may not be from the same person)" is a business philosophy that many successful people subscribe to. This networking strategy will help you get what you want because others will see you as someone who:

- cares about more than just your own success
- is interested in others and wants to help them succeed
- understands the concept of "one hand washes the other"

How do you know what others need? Before you offer your wonderful products, services, skills, and knowledge, first ask, "What are your greatest challenges right now?" or "Who are your typical clients?" Then be an active listener and probe the areas where you may be able to provide some assistance or expertise. Then you can say, "After what you've told me, I may be able to help you with . . ."

E *in the Word* T-A-R-G-E-T = Expand *Your Sphere of Influence*

To a certain degree, networking is a numbers game, and you can get the odds working in your favor by helping as many people as possible make connections for their mutual benefit. To expand your sphere of influence at a networking event, learn as much as you can beforehand about the attendees so you know who might have common interests and goals. Plus, consider doing the following:

- act as a host to make attendees, especially newcomers, feel welcome and comfortable
- introduce targeted attendees to other people of influence
- integrate targeted attendees into group conversations
- work the room to make sure that all attendees are engaged and networking.

T *in the Word* T-A-R-G-E-T = Time *Your Conversations at the* Networking Event

Have you missed connecting with someone you wanted to talk to at an event because you chatted too long with someone else? Making the most of every networking opportunity at an event depends, in large part, on how well you manage your time. How long you spend networking with each person depends on several factors, including the person's status, his or her availability, the scope of your conversation, and your networking goals. One way to estimate how much time to spend networking with each person is to consider this formula:

$$\frac{\text{Time you have to network}}{\text{Number of people to talk to}} = \text{Networking time per person}$$

For example, if you have about an hour to network and you want to connect with between six and ten people, you've got about five to ten minutes of networking time per person. The trick is to be flexible, yet also manage your time. Here's what you can say to gracefully end the conversation and move on:

> *We obviously have lots to talk about, but I know you are here to network too. Plus, I need to say hello to some other people here before they leave. So, can I give you a call in the next few days to continue our conversation?*

Or, you might offer:

> *I'm glad we got a chance to talk. I've enjoyed hearing about your . . . I'm going to say hello to some colleagues here, but before I do, I'd be happy to introduce you to some other people I know here.*

FAQ

I'm great at starting conversations and networking. It's the follow-up where I drop the ball. What can I do?

Do You Suffer from LAF (Lack of Follow-up)?

Many networkers fail to follow up with any consistency. However, little or nothing will come from your networking efforts without following up. Here are three simple yet effective ways to follow up and continue the conversations you started while networking at an event. Timing is critical, so make contact within a few days of your last conversation.

1. Send a short e-mail. The easiest follow-up is a brief and friendly email. It says that you enjoyed your last encounter and want to continue the exchange. For example:

> *I enjoyed meeting you at . . . and especially chatting about . . . I'm wondering if you'd like to continue our conversation. If so, let me know when you have a few minutes to talk and I'll give you a call.*

2. Call on the telephone. A short telephone conversation is a convenient and personal way to follow up with a networking contact. Whether you talk to the person directly or leave a voice mail, always identify yourself, remind the person where you met, and say something like:

> *I wanted to give you a quick call to say how much I enjoyed chatting with you about . . . Also, if you have a few minutes, I found the information you asked me about. If now isn't convenient, let me know a good time to call you and I'll get back to you.*

3. Ask for a short meeting. Meeting briefly in person is a personal and time-conscious way to follow up with someone you've previously met and talked to at a networking event. Making the time short and convenient will encourage the person to agree. You can ask:

> *I'd really like to hear more about how you . . . Will you have time for a quick cup of coffee or something to drink before or after our meeting next week?*

If both of you are willing to invest more time, then suggest meeting over lunch or even dinner. Remember, good etiquette says that the person who offers the invitation to dine picks up the bill!

Three Keys to Following Up: Keep It Simple, Keep It Sincere, Keep It Consistent

The way to follow up and get the biggest return on your networking investment is to:

1. Keep it simple. Well-written e-mails and text messages (if they are not full of typos), phone calls, and short meetings allow you to maintain contact without a huge investment of time.

2. Keep it sincere. Offers to help and delivering on your promises build trust, rapport, and goodwill. All this will come back to you because you are building a relationship.

3. Keep it consistent. Maintaining communication without spamming or hounding keeps you and your contacts aligned and in tune with each other so that each time you meet and talk, your relationship will grow for your mutual benefit.

And that, after all, is what networking is all about!

14

Making New Friends and Rekindling Old Friendships

If I don't have friends, then I ain't got nothin'.
—Billie Holiday (1915–1959), jazz singer

The Gift of Lifelong Friendship

Every spring for the last fifteen years, a dozen guys I grew up with from elementary, junior high, and high school—collectively known as the ESB, or Eastside Boys—meet for a boys-only weekend reunion. We just hang out, catch up on family and career news (some good, some not so good), play cards, eat, tell and retell old stories, and add some new ones too. What makes our time together so special to all of us is that we have known each other for such a long time and we still have a few times a year to keep the connections strong. When we do meet, our old friendships kick in right where we left off. I strive to maintain these lifelong friendships with my ESB buddies because these good friends improve the quality of my life.

Making friends is a goal if we value companionship. Most people have only a few friends whom they trust completely with their most personal feelings and information. When you give someone your friendship, it becomes an important aspect of a relationship. Unfortunately, there are many who feel they have no one to confide in and call a good friend. This can change, because good friendships can begin at any stage in your life.

What Is Friendship?

It has been said that love is blind, and friendship is just not noticing. Friends can be allies, supporters, or sympathizers. They give encouragement, feedback, honest opinions, and a lot of advice. We reveal things to friends that we just wouldn't tell anyone else. A friend is someone we can trust with sensitive information and know that he or she won't hold it against us. A friend is also someone who shares common interests and experiences with us and adds to our sense of fulfillment. Other elements of good friendship are:

patience	stimulation	sympathy	intimacy
respect	equality	fun	spontaneity
understanding	reliability	flexibility	another view
sharing	helping	enrichment	compassion
learning	freedom	tolerance	trust
companionship	love	reassurance	honesty

Making Friends Is Not Always Easy

Making friends takes time, effort, commitment, give-and-take, and a lot of tolerance for the many human frailties we all have. Although most people put a high priority on their families and careers, you can find and make good friends at any stage of your life.

To Make New Friends, Go Where You Have Fun

There are countless places to meet people, and there is little doubt that some places are better than others, especially to make contact with potential friends. The "right place" could be a social event, your place of worship, a political gathering, or even an adult education class. When you meet someone in a place where you both enjoy the activities, you already have something in common and can begin developing a friendship.

Making and Keeping Friends Rest on Four Key Principles

- Take the initiative and reach out to others.

- Show genuine interest in people.

- Treat others with respect and kindness.

- Value yourself and others as unique individuals who have much to offer.

Meet People Who Have Similar Interests

Suppose you are a beginning photographer who likes to travel into the countryside to shoot pictures. You have just bought a new camera, so you decide to sign up for a beginning photography class. At the photography class, you will meet other people with at least one thing in common: photography. Many of your early conversations will probably focus around this topic and other, related fields. Start your conversations by finding out the different reasons others are taking the class. You can ask questions like "What do you hope to gain from this class?" and "How long have you been taking photographs?" and "How did you become interested in photography?" As you talk, you can get a sense of whether you and the other person enjoy each other's company. If so, you may have started a new friendship.

New Friendships Can Begin Anywhere

Think of all the people you meet and see at work, in your neighborhood, and especially at recreational or social events you attend. Many are potential friends, and you can develop relationships with them. When you see the same people over a period of time in your neighborhood, at work, or at the Laundromat, start conversations. Find out if you have something in common. If the conditions are right, start up a friendship. Begin by smiling and saying hello and, if the opportunity arises, introducing yourself and showing that you are open to contact.

Keep Your Contact Friendly and Informal

After you have said hello a few times, you will most likely find an opportunity to stop and chat for a few moments. Maybe it's at work, while walking down the street, or in the local food store. Show the other person that you are interested in getting to know him better by engaging in casual conversation. You don't have to be profound or too impressive. It's better to be informal, friendly, and receptive. Remember: Small talk sends the signal "I'm interested in you, and open to conversation. Let's talk!" Small talk also gives people an opportunity to ask themselves, *Do I want to get to know this person better?*

Don't Wait to Introduce Yourself

When there is a pause in a beginning conversation, take the opportunity to say, "By the way, my name is . . . What's yours?" The sooner you introduce yourself, the easier it is. Remember, the longer you wait to make an introduction, the more uncomfortable it can get.

Quickly Zero In on "Hot Buttons"

The sooner you find out what turns someone on, the sooner you'll be able to establish whether you have anything in common. Sometimes you will know about a person before you actually meet. Remember to look for objects that the person carries, such as shopping bags with store logos, musical instruments, sports equipment, tools, building supplies—anything that might give you a clue to the person's hot button. Then ask, "I saw you walking the other day with . . . Do you like to . . . ?"

Keep an Inventory of Facts and Details about the Person

When you talk to someone a second or third time, recall information from a previous conversation: he or she will be surprised and flattered. Comments like "How's the job hunt going?" and "How's your garden coming along?" will show the other person that you were actually listening and that you care about what's happening in his or her life. This makes the person feel good—and important. Be sure to concentrate on the details that someone discloses to you, and make a point to remember key words and free information from the conversation. You'll be able to draw on this reservoir of information to sustain and direct later conversations.

Be Available to Chat

When you want to get to know someone better, make it a point to stop and chat when the opportunities present themselves. This will reinforce a friendly, outgoing attitude and send the signal that you want to learn more about him or her. Your attention demonstrates your interest and curiosity, and encourages others to talk and reveal more information. When people begin to open up, it shows they are gaining trust in you and are comfortable with you. This may be the beginning of a friendship.

Caution: Take care not to come on too strong to someone you have recently met. Be casual, informal, and comfortable. Take it slow and easy, and don't be pushy or aggressive.

Extending a Casual Invitation Says, "I'd Like to Get to Know You Better"

During casual conversation with someone you want to become better acquainted with, suggest going out for some casual conversation over a drink, coffee, or ice cream, or during any other informal activity. This shows you like the person and want to get to know her better. If the person is available and receptive, chances are she may say, "Sure, why not!" Make an attempt to set a particular day and time by saying, "What's a good day and time for you?" or "How's tonight?" or "When's good for you?"

After you've had a few comfortable conversations with the person, you can extend a casual invitation to join you in a short related activity. For example, you can say:

To a coworker: "I usually get a quick lunch at a little restaurant a few blocks away from work. You can join me sometime if you like."

To a neighbor: "I'm going to the hardware store to get some plants (building supplies, etc.). Do you want to come along?"

To a member of a club or organization: "I also belong to . . . Would you like to come to one of our meetings as my guest?"

FAQ

I'm at work talking to a friend. I want to have dinner with him, but I'm afraid to ask. What should I do?

Getting someone to share a meal with you isn't really so difficult when you figure nearly everybody eats at least one meal daily. When you are speaking to someone you already know slightly, at work or in any other situation, keep your ears open for a "food" hot button. It's easy to introduce the subject into conversation by merely asking questions about nearby restaurants, particular favorite foods, or memorable meals. Say: "Do you know any good restaurants around here?" or "How is the food at the restaurant on the corner?" or "Have you ever been to Louie's? I hear the food there is excellent!"

Once you establish that you have some similar tastes in food, then suggest, "How about meeting for dinner one night next week after work? I know a great little place with great food and a fantastic atmosphere." Usually, if someone wants to spend time with you, he or she will accept your open invitation. Now it's up to you to focus on a specific day and time. "What are you doing for dinner tonight? Are you interested in joining me for a bite to eat?" or "What kind of food do you like?" is an easy way to ask someone to share a meal with you. If you expect to be taken out for dinner, then you will have to wait for an invitation. If you go dutch treat, there are no expectations attached, and either party can initiate the date.

Plan an Activity around a Mutual Interest

After you spend some time together informally, propose sharing a longer activity you know the other person likes to do, and one that you are interested in too. It could be going to a movie, bike riding, attending a sports event, or going out for lunch. It won't matter as long as the event is mutually interesting and the focus is on fun. Presenting a few options and suggesting a time within the next week or so will increase the likelihood of a positive response. Your invitation could open with something like: "I remember when we talked before that you said you liked (the activity), so I was wondering, are you interested in joining me for . . .

. . . dinner one night this week?"
. . . a movie this weekend?"
. . . Sunday's baseball game?"
. . . an art exhibition Thursday at the museum?"
. . . a few sets of tennis after work?"
. . . a walk on the beach?"
. . . a bike ride?"
. . . a class on the Internet?"

A Telephone Call Is a Warm Way to Confirm a Meeting

Give your friend a call to confirm the time of your planned meeting, and just to say hello. Although some people prefer to confirm meetings via e-mail, a telephone conversation can be a warmer exchange. Here are some tips for more comfortable telephone conversations.

- Get into a comfortable position, preferably seated.

- When the person answers the phone, always identify yourself. *Never play "Guess who this is."* Say, "Hi, . . . , this is . . . . Have you got a few minutes to talk?"

- Tell the other person why you are calling: "I just wanted to confirm our meeting," or "I just thought I'd call to say hi."

- Follow up with a question about some aspect of the person's life, like "How's your big project coming along?" or "How did your blind date turn out?"

- End your telephone call with a friendly comment like "It's been nice talking with you," or "We'll be talking again soon," or "I'm looking forward to getting together with you on Saturday."

Be Open to New Experiences with Others

When a new friend asks you to join an activity, make an all-out effort to accept the invitation. This reinforces the other person's feelings of friendship toward you and encourages her to share her experiences and activities. Let your friends introduce you to new places, new people, new food, or anything else they want to share. This shows openness and receptivity to your friends' ideas and allows them to feel good about sharing things they enjoy. This attitude also creates a positive feeling toward you, and your friends will become more receptive to the ideas and activities you suggest.

How to Decline an Invitation

Sometimes conflicting schedules or other reasons may prevent you from accepting an invitation from a new friend. However, if you say, "I'm not in the mood," or "I really don't feel like it," your response translates as disinterest. If you decline or try to reschedule too many invitations, the other person will get the message that you're not interested in getting together.

To let the person know that you still want to spend time with him or her, you can say something like "I'd love to, but I'm busy on . . . Can we make it for another day next week?" Or to reschedule a planned get-together, you can say something like "I'm sorry I have to do this, but I need to reschedule our . . . for . . . How does . . . work for you? It'll be my treat. Again, I apologize."

Always return invitations and ask your friends to share in activities that you enjoy too. Make an effort to share some of the special places and events that interest you. Friendly gestures like these show others you like them and, at the same time, help them learn about your likes and passions.

Developing Trust

Friendships take time to develop because they require mutual trust between people, and trust takes time to develop. To gain someone's trust, you must reveal some personal information and feelings so that the other person can gain a real sense of what kind of person you are. As time goes on, you and your friends will disclose more and more personal information, and the trust between you will grow. In the early stages of friendship, people don't always know how much to reveal. If you balance the information being traded back and forth, then your rate of self-disclosure is probably appropriate.

A firm belief in someone's honesty and reliability takes time to develop, while a breach of trust can destroy a relationship instantly. When a friend confides in you, keep the information to yourself if you value the friendship.

Friendships Grow and Develop in Time

Friendships are like plants: they grow slowly and steadily in time. Your friendship will become stronger as you share more experiences together. To show your appreciation for a longtime friend, you can say:

We've been good friends for a long time.
We've gone through some pretty amazing times together.
I don't know what I would have done without you.
Thanks for all the help and support you've given me during the
    last couple of months. It's really made a big difference, and I
    appreciate it a lot.
I've really enjoyed the last few months that we've worked
    together.

To tell a new friend that you enjoy spending time together,
you can say,

We've got to do this more often.
You're a fun person to be around.
I'm glad we got to know each other better.

FAQ

I'm with an old friend whom I haven't seen for a long time.
Where does the conversation begin?

How to Rekindle a Friendship

Recently I got a phone call: "Hey, is this Don? This is a blast from
your past. It's Andy P. Remember me? We all played in a band
together twenty years ago!" I immediately recognized the friendly
voice on the telephone.

After chatting comfortably for a few minutes Andy and I agreed
to meet a few days later to catch up. We had a great time and it
was as if we'd never lost touch. Since then we have met several
more times with our wives: for dinner in their home, for a barbe-
cue in my backyard, for city exploring and jazz concerts. And all
this happened because Andy decided one day to pick up the telephone and call me for no reason other than to say hello. And I'm
glad that he did, because now our friendship is back on track and
going strong.

Be a "Blast from the Past"

Whether you've been out of touch for ten, fifteen, twenty-five, or
even fifty years, it's never too late to rekindle a friendship. All it
takes is:

- a telephone call (like the one from Andy to me)
- a short e-mail or handwritten note
- a reintroduction at a class reunion
- a chance meeting at a social or business get-together
- a search on Facebook, MySpace, LinkedIn, or other social networking sites
- a visit to the neighborhood where you grew up or the place you worked
- a mutual friend who may know the whereabouts of another old buddy.

Breaking the Ice with a Long-Lost Friend

"What have you been doing all these years?" is probably the most frequently asked question old friends ask and one that you need to be ready to answer. You can say something like: "For the last several years I've been living (with my . . .) and working as a . . . (owning my own business, going to school, retired, etc.). What about you?"

However, be brief with the details and ask what your old friend has been up to, too. You can talk more about the specifics once you've caught up on the bigger events in each other's lives.

Handling Sensitive Questions

"Are you (still) married?" and "How's the family?" are questions that inevitably come up during catch-up chats with old friends. However, for obvious reasons, they can lead to embarrassing or uncomfortable silences, so consider replacing them with general questions that give the other person the choice of how much or little to say: "Do you live alone or with someone?" or "And what are your kids up to these days?" or "How's your business (job) going?"

If you are divorced or widowed you can say something like "I've been divorced for years," or "I'm sad to say that I lost my husband (wife) . . . years ago."

If you have health, financial, job, or other personal problems, it's best to omit them from your conversation in the early stages of rekindling a friendship. If you start complaining about your problems, it will appear as though you are hoping your friend can solve them for you.

Mending a Fractured Friendship

Sometimes friends can lose contact for years over thoughtless words, a disagreement, or a misunderstanding, but it doesn't have to remain that way. If you want to reconcile with an old friend, then consider being the one to hold out an olive branch. Take the initiative to reach out with a letter, e-mail, or telephone call. Whether or not you are at fault, apologize for your part that led to the breach, and you may find that your old friend will do the same. Here is what you can say to get past a past argument with an old friend: "I want to apologize for . . . I was wrong and I'm sorry. Our friendship means a lot to me, and if you are willing, I'd like to let bygones be bygones."

"The Only Way to Have a Friend Is to Be One"—Ralph Waldo Emerson

It has been said that a friend knows all about you but likes you anyway. To remain friends and nurture friendships, you need to be flexible and tolerant. Accept your friends as unique individuals with the problems, hang-ups, and inconsistencies that all humans possess. If you accept your friends on these conditions, you will be much more likely to keep them. When a friend asks you for a favor, do it if you possibly can. Your friends will do the same for you. If you are a good friend, you'll have good friends. Developing and learning together is one of the most gratifying aspects of a relationship. In the best friendships, developing, learning, and laughing never stop.

15

Talking with Confidence
on First Dates

I don't know the question, but sex is definitely the answer.
—Woody Allen (1935–), American screenwriter, film director,
actor, comedian, writer, musician, and playwright

University researchers Drs. Raymond Fisman, Sheena Iyengar, Emir Kamenica, and Itamar Simonson created a study on how people chose potential dates when attending speed-dating events. Their findings revealed that during a five-minute meeting, the participants made up their minds about possible people whom they wanted to date in less than a minute. In other words, first impressions really do count! In addition, they found that regarding preferences, "women put a greater weight on intelligence than men do, while men place more value on physical appearance." Their research also suggested that in many instances men and women chose people whom they considered similar to themselves in social status.

Whatever the reasons for going on a first date, there's no question that it can be nerve-racking, especially if you haven't been dating for a while or are new to the task. Of course, it can be exciting, too, especially when you sense some chemistry between the two of you, even though initially you might feel a little shy or uncomfortable. How do you get to know each other without your first date sounding like a job interview? How do you know what and what *not* to talk about? How do you handle personal or embarrassing issues? That's where your conversation skills can really help you and your date get to know each other and feel at ease. Plus, the information that you exchange will help you determine if the two of you have enough in common to have a second or third date and, perhaps, even begin a romantic relationship.

The Beginning of a First Date: Getting the Conversation Going and Setting the Right Tone

Whether your first date is with someone you know, someone you've just met, or a blind date, your initial exchanges set the tone for what is to follow. Of course, what you say is important, but *how* you say it—that is, your body language and tone of voice—have a huge impact on how each of you feels and the first impressions you make. Therefore, when you first meet, be sure to smile, offer a warm and friendly—not a businesslike—handshake, and make plenty of eye contact. Immediately tune in to your date's body language and tone of voice. If your date appears especially friendly, you can venture a small kiss on the cheek in addition to or in lieu of a handshake. This initial extra bit of intimacy when you first meet can put both of you more at ease and set a warm tone for the rest of your date.

Balance Talking and Listening to Overcome Early Jitters

If you feel a little shy or nervous at the beginning of a first date, don't worry. That's natural and will pass. The trick to getting past the awkward early moments of a first date is to engage in light conversation, or small talk. This gives you an opportunity to get settled and establish a quick conversational flow back and forth. Be sure you balance the amount of time you talk and listen. Small talk also allows you to share experiences, background information, and preferences that open the way for deeper and more insightful conversation. However, in the first few minutes, keep your conversational topics light and upbeat. Talk and ask about topics that evoke both of your passions and interests. Don't get too serious, complain about anything, or bring up unpleasant news or subjects.

Quickly Exchange Background and Some Personal Information

As your first date gets going, both of you will want to learn more personal details about each other. You don't need to wait to be asked about certain personal information. You can reveal it through self-disclosures, but do so sparingly and at about an equal rate as your date. Sprinkle into your conversation this kind of personal background information to reveal more details about yourself. This indicates trust and helps guide the conversation to a deeper level. The more personal the disclosures, the greater the trust. To trade small amounts of ritual, or basic, background information, you can reveal something about yourself and then say, "What about you?"

Ritual information includes topics and self-disclosures such as:

- **Where you are from and your family situation:** "I grew up in . . . I'm an only child. What about you?"
- **What brought you to where you are today:** "I moved here in . . . to go to school. After graduating, I got a job and I've been here ever since! What about you?"
- **Your vocation and hobbies:** "I enjoy working as a . . . For recreation I love to . . . What about you?"
- **What you studied and where you went to school:** "I studied . . . and graduated from . . . in the year . . . What about you?"
- **Your religion:** "I was raised a . . . and worship at . . . What about you?"
- **Some family history:** "My father was raised in . . . My mother grew up in . . . I was born in . . . What about you?"
- **Where you want to go from here:** "My next big goal is to . . . What about you?"

Listening between the Lines Is Your Guide to Deeper Conversation

Another conversation goal of a first date is to find out which, if any, values and attitudes you share. While more outgoing people come right out and tell others about what's important to them, more reserved people may prefer to imply their feelings, opinions, and attitudes. Listen between the lines of conversation for these kinds of implied statements. Then show interest by asking open-ended follow-up questions that probe deeper for the motivations and feelings behind the statements. Generally, if your date makes an implied statement, it suggests that, if asked, he or she may be willing to talk about that topic. Here are some examples of questions that will elicit more detailed responses based on implied or indirect statements:

> *From what you just said, it sounds like there is more to the story.*
> *I'd like to hear more about that.*
> *It sounds like you had some other reasons, too, for choosing . . . .*
> *Am I right?*
> *You seem to imply that you are . . . Am I correct?*
> *I'm not sure that I understand what you mean by . . . Can you*
> *give me an example?*
> *After listening to you describe . . . I'm wondering: How did you*
> *arrive at that conclusion?*

A Good Sense of Humor Makes You More Desirable

According to a study published in the *Journal of Psychology*, researchers Elizabeth McGee and Mark Shevlin concluded "people with a good sense of humor received significantly higher ratings of attractiveness and suitability than do those with an average or no sense of humor." The study just shows what average-looking folks have hoped for all along: you don't need to be a model or a perfect "10" to be desirable. Just showing your sense of humor and making people laugh makes them feel comfortable. As a result, they will like you and want to be with you.

Showing your sense of humor doesn't mean that you have to be a stand-up comic or tell one-liners. You can share an amusing or embarrassing experience, something funny you read, saw on television, or in a movie, or observed on the street that gave you a chuckle. What makes you laugh is a direct reflection of how you see the world. By the same token, laughing (not giggling) at things your date says acknowledges that you share his or her definition of what's funny. And this, according to another study on humor conducted by B. I. Murstein and R. G. Brust in the *Journal of Personality Assessment*, may prove the point. They also found that "[participants] with a good sense of humor received significantly higher ratings of attractiveness and suitability than those with an average or no sense of humor." That's a pretty good reason to show your sense of humor and see if your date laughs.

FAQ

I dine at a local restaurant where I often see someone else who usually eats alone. How can I ask her if she wants to join me for dinner?

Make an effort to be seated near the person dining alone, and when she looks in your direction, make eye contact, nod, and smile. If she smiles back, you can say, "Hello. I've noticed that you eat here a lot too. What are you having for dinner tonight?" Remember that you are just showing interest and seeing if she appears open for contact. If her response is friendly, you might say, "I really like their sandwiches here, but tonight I feel like something different. What do you usually order?" The goal is to start a conversation from your separate seats and see where it leads. If it seems like she wants to continue to talk, you can say, "If you're not waiting for someone, would you like to join me?" or "Do you mind if I join you?"

Many people who frequently dine alone might be happy to accept your invitation if you approach them in a friendly and low-pressure way. You can also offer to buy a person a drink to show you are interested in chatting with her. Just remember that your offer is only a friendly gesture. It doesn't necessarily mean that you are treating her to dinner or that she owes you anything in return. However, if she declines your invitation, she may be shy or she might simply prefer her own company. Don't get upset or angry. Just smile and say, "No problem, maybe some other time. Enjoy your meal."

How Do You Ask a Personal Question?

Asking a personal question always requires a particular sensitivity to the other person's feelings, and especially his level of receptivity to you. It is usually best to preface personal questions with a softener, like "Excuse me for asking but . . ." or "I'd love to know, if you don't mind telling me . . . ?" or "I hope I'm not being too personal, but . . . ?" or "If you don't mind my asking . . . ?"

If you ask a personal question in such a way that the other person does not have to answer, often he will respond in some form. It may not be the direct answer you are looking for, because many people have trouble saying what they really mean, especially if it's about a sensitive topic. However, if you listen carefully for free information and look for receptive body language, you can get an indication whether the person trusts you enough to reveal some personal information.

Asking Questions That Focus on Relationships Can Lead to Better Matches

At some point during the middle of your first date, you're probably going to exchange some of your opinions, experiences, and attitudes regarding personal relationships. After all, this is a topic that concerns most singles seriously looking for a mate and can dictate the likelihood of future dates and the success of a long-term relationship. Many dating experts agree that the sooner two people know each other's preferences regarding personal relationships, the better. However, this is a sensitive area, so initially keep your questions and answers general. Tread lightly, especially if you sense any hesitation. Here are some questions that will elicit some basic attitudes and views on this subject. You can see if your date is open to the discussion with a question like:

> *We've chatted about lots of different subjects, but I'd like to ask you about something more personal regarding how you feel about relationships. Are you open to that?*
> *What are you looking for in a relationship?*
> *What is it that you want most from a partner?*
> *How would you describe a good relationship?*
> *What's the longest relationship you've been in?*

If the other person is reluctant to talk about relationships on your first date, don't push it. You can offer your views and then change the topic to something less personal and bring it up at another time. However, you and your date's responses to these questions reveal important personal goals and values, so don't let them go unanswered for too long.

Bringing Up the Big Issues on a First Date

I remember when I was single chatting over a cup of coffee with a woman on a first date. After we had spent a polite few minutes exchanging some background information and what we liked to do in our spare time, she quickly brought up a subject important to her: religion. It didn't take long after that for us to conclude that this was our first and last date. People interested in pursuing a long-term relationship usually want to know some critical information about each other before getting too involved. These issues may be difficult to discuss on a first date, but the longer you wait to bring them up, the harder they can be to talk about. Whether you discuss them on your first date or soon after, you'll want to know:

- **Current relationship status (be honest if you want to be trusted):**
  You can ask: "Are you currently involved with someone?"
  You can disclose: "I'm dating, but not seeing anyone special."

- **Prior relationships (this has to do with commitment and family responsibilities):**
  You can ask: "Have you ever been married or been in a long-term relationship? Do you have any kids?"
  You can disclose: "I was married (living with . . .) for . . . years. I (don't) have kids.

- **Religion (for some people this is a critical issue; for others it's not):**
  You can ask: "Were you raised in a particular religion?"
  You can disclose: "I'm (not, sort of, quite) religious."

- **Politics (for some people this is a critical issue; for others it's not):**
  You can ask: "Who did you vote for (support) in the last presidential election?"
  You can disclose: "I belong to the . . . Party and I would say my political views are generally (liberal, moderate, or conservative)."

- **Health (for most people this is a critical issue, especially where sex is concerned):**
  You can ask: "I know this is really personal, but do you have any health issues I should know about if we are going to see each other?"
  You can disclose: "This is kind of personal, but I have a health issue that I want to tell you about if we are going to date."

- **Sex (discussing sexual attitudes is personal and can make some people feel uncomfortable):**
  You can ask: "Do you mind if I ask you a personal question about sex?"
  You can disclose: "This is kind of personal with regard to my attitude on sex, but I want you to know that . . ."

Ten Things Not to Say on a First Date

Don't blow your first date by saying:

1. "My cell never stops ringing. I'm on call 24/7."
2. "Let me tell you about my last blind date."
3. "That's something my ex would have said."
4. "If you're not going to finish that, can I have the rest?"
5. "I have a headache to die for."
6. "I just got out of rehab."
7. "My family has a history of . . ."
8. "I don't want to sound like I'm bragging but . . ."
9. "Why did you and your ex break up?"
10. "I think sex on a first date is a cool thing, don't you?"

The Middle of Your First Date: "How Do You Like Me So Far?"

You may be about midway through your first date, so it's time to do a reality check. If you are chatting easily about a variety of general subjects, laughing, discovering more common interests, experiences, and especially personal goals and values, then you are well on your way to a second date. However, if your date isn't going as well as you had hoped, you still have time to turn things around.

Calling 911: Ten Bad Signs That You Need Help on a First Date

Bad Sign #1: Closed Body Language

911 response: A date can't read your mind, but he or she can read your closed body language, and the message is not good. Uncross your arms, smile, increase your eye contact, and lean closer to show you want to send a more friendly and positive message. If your date's body language is closed, then try this "monkey see, monkey do" technique: *Briefly* mirror his or her closed body language. Then, after a few moments, slowly unfold your arms, lean forward slightly, and smile. Hopefully, your date will mirror your open body language.

Bad Sign #2: Talking Incessantly or Speaking Very Little

911 response: If you are talking more than 50 percent of the time, stop. Ask open-ended questions, let your date speak—without interruption—and listen. If you are silent more than 50 percent of the time, talk more. Reveal more about your background, what you like, your goals, and what makes you laugh. Let your date know more about you and what you are willing to talk about.

Bad Sign #3: Tuning Out

911 response: Pay attention, listen, and respond. Ask follow-up questions for more details, suggest examples, share insights, and make related comments based on what your date says.

Bad Sign #4: Showing Little Emotion or Enthusiasm

911 response: Wake up! Smile, laugh, ask questions, and share comments to get involved in the conversation to show you are interested in your date's experiences and views.

Bad Sign #5: Long Periods of Silence

911 response: Kick-start the conversation with "You said something earlier that reminded me of a similar experience (piqued my curiosity, etc.)," or "You mentioned that you . . . I'd love to hear more about that."

Bad Sign #6: Cell Phone Interruptions

911 response: Turn off your cell phone and leave it off. If not, let your date know that you are "on call" and may be interrupted but that you'll keep the calls as short as possible. Give your date your full attention. If your date is tied to his or her cell phone, you can ask with a smile, "Maybe you can turn off your cell or put it on vibrate so we can get to know each other a little without being interrupted every few minutes."

Bad Sign #7: Disagreeing about Politics, Religion, or Other Issues Great or Small

911 response: End a contentious discussion *before* it turns into an argument and change the subject. You might say, "I can see that we don't see eye to eye on this, so how about we just agree to disagree and leave it at that. I want to change the subject. Can I tell you about a new project I have coming up?"

Bad Sign #8: Revealing Too Much or Too Little Personal Information

911 response: Failing to reveal basic personal information suggests a lack of trust or something to hide. Revealing too much personal information too soon can make you appear needy or desperate. Open up a little at a time and share something significant about yourself that tells your date who you are. You can say, "Here are a few things about me that will give you an idea of what makes me tick."

Bad Sign #9: Frequently Checking the Time

911 response: Glancing at your watch more than a few times during a first date implies that you are eager for it to be over. If you need to know the time for a particular reason, let your date know why so he or she doesn't think that you want to be somewhere else.

Bad Sign #10: Conversation That Sounds Like a Job Interview

911 response: Lighten up, share a few laughs, and get to know each other. A date is to have fun and see if there is interest to pursue a relationship. You and your date are not applying for a job.

Ending Your First Date

As your first date comes to a close, how do you end it with the best shot at getting a second date? Since people usually remember more how they feel at the end of their first date than any other time, it's important to make your last topic of conversation upbeat so you can leave a good and lasting impression. If you want to meet again, use the final few minutes of your conversation to make your case. Granted, this is a tense moment. It takes a bit of courage to speak your mind and be up front about what you want.

This shows that you are confident and know how to tactfully assert yourself—a quality that most people admire. If you want to see your date again, be direct and say so. For example: "This date was fun. I'd like to go out with you again. How about it?" or "I really enjoyed spending this time with you. Would you like to join me for a movie or dinner next weekend?" or "Shall we do this again?" or "I'm up to go out again, if you are."

Saying No with a "Soft" Rejection

You have the right to decline an invitation to a second date, but there is no need to crush the other person's feelings and self-esteem in the process. However, a lame excuse such as "I'm so busy with my job that I can't date right now," or a condescending remark such as "You're really a nice person, but . . ." certainly don't make people feel less rejected. It's best to be polite, direct, and brief. You can say something like "It's nice of you to ask, but I'm going to say no," or "Thanks for asking, but I'm going to pass."

Accept a Rejection and Move On

Rejections! No one likes them and they do hurt your pride. However, everyone who dates gets rejected at one time or another, so it's not the end of the world if your invitation for a second date gets turned down. Just accept it gracefully. Don't argue, ask why, or pressure your date to change his or her mind. That will only cause embarrassment and can easily lead to a humiliating or unpleasant exchange—at your expense. It's best to say something like "I enjoyed our date, but I respect your decision. I appreciate you being direct with me."

A Successful Conversation = A Successful First Date

In the end, the key to a successful first date is a successful conversation. You and your date had a good time together and felt good about yourselves and each other. You exchanged enough background and personal information that you felt comfortable opening up and sharing even more personal details of your lives. You discovered common interests and values that will be the basis of future conversations and will allow you to have more meaningful exchanges. Finally, you've created rapport, trust, and a sense of optimism that this date was just the first of many more to come.

16

Recognizing and Using Conversation Styles

> New Yorkers, by reputation, are fast-talking, assertive and easily annoyed; I fit right in.
> —Jane Pauley (1950–), American television journalist

Do some of your conversations start with a bang, while others sputter out after a few uncomfortable moments? Once you begin talking, do some of your chats flow smoothly from topic to topic, while others degenerate into heated disagreements? Is it a mystery why one discussion is fun and stimulating, while another is interminably boring? Are some folks just easier to talk to than others? In a nutshell, are your conversations something like playing roulette in that you're never sure if you are going to come out a winner or a loser?

One way to minimize conversational ups and downs is to recognize and use conversation styles. Most people have a primary conversation style that loosely falls into one of four categories. (You'll know your conversation style after you take the short self-assessment on the next few pages.) By identifying your own style, plus recognizing the strengths and weaknesses of each of the four styles, you can feel more comfortable while talking to almost anyone. You will see how quickly you can create rapport and skillfully converse with nearly everyone you meet, no matter how different his or her style is from yours. Besides building your confidence, you can mingle more easily with groups, quickly find common ground with strangers, and make plenty of new friends.

What's Your Conversation Style?

Answer the following questions to identify your primary conversation style. Choose the letter that best describes how you truly behave—not how you'd like to behave—in each situation.

1. **When I enter a roomful of strangers, I:**
   - ☐ a. mingle and observe interesting discussions. ♠
   - ☐ b. introduce myself to the first stranger I meet. ♥
   - ☐ c. sit in a chair and wait for someone to approach me. ♦
   - ☐ d. look for a "friendly debate." ♣

2. **When I meet people for the first time, I:**
   - ☐ a. quickly form my opinions of them. ♠
   - ☐ b. tell them about myself before I ask my questions. ♣
   - ☐ c. try to make them laugh. ♥
   - ☐ d. play it cool and see what they do. ♦

3. **When I am engaged in conversation, I:**
   - ☐ a. let others share their opinions before I offer my own. ♦
   - ☐ b. listen for holes in the other person's opinions. ♠
   - ☐ c. get my point across as quickly as I can. ♣
   - ☐ d. ask questions and share my views. ♥

4. **If I am uninformed about a topic of conversation, I:**
   - ☐ a. nod silently and try to look interested. ♦
   - ☐ b. change the subject. ♥
   - ☐ c. ask questions to show interest. ♠
   - ☐ d. pretend like I know what I'm talking about. ♣

5. **If I disagree with another person's views, I:**
   - ☐ a. like to discuss the reasons behind his opinion. ♥
   - ☐ b. say very little. ♦
   - ☐ c. vigorously press my opinion. ♣
   - ☐ d. explain point by point why he is wrong. ♠

6.   I prefer conversations that are:
- [ ] a.   to the point. ♣
- [ ] b.   factual and detailed. ♠
- [ ] c.   oriented around "small talk." ♥
- [ ] d.   personal. ♦

7.   I like conversations that allow me to:
- [ ] a.   learn about others. ♦
- [ ] b.   be the center of attention. ♥
- [ ] c.   explain complicated concepts. ♠
- [ ] d.   tell others what I have accomplished. ♣

8.   Which statement best describes you?
- [ ] a.   I can make "small talk" about a variety of subjects. ♥
- [ ] b.   I can zero in on the core issue of a topic. ♣
- [ ] c.   I can listen so that others will open up to me. ♦
- [ ] d.   I can explain difficult concepts. ♠

9.   The people who I find hardest to talk with are those who:
- [ ] a.   push their opinions on me. ♦
- [ ] b.   speak nonstop without letting anyone else get a word in edgewise. ♠
- [ ] c.   get hung up on every little detail. ♣
- [ ] d.   give complex explanations. ♥

10.   My favorite conversations are the ones in which I:
- [ ] a.   tell a funny story. ♥
- [ ] b.   discuss a technical topic. ♠
- [ ] c.   present a viewpoint. ♣
- [ ] d.   listen to others open up. ♦

Scoring

Count the number of responses with each of the symbols (♣, ♦, ♠, ♥). The style with the highest number of responses is probably closest to your conversation style. Most people are a combination of styles with one or sometimes two primary styles. Since there are ten questions, your total will add up to 10.

For example

♣	6	Candid
♦	0	Humble
♠	1	Accurate
♥	3	Talkative

Total   10

Your scores

♣	_____	Candid
♦	_____	Humble
♠	_____	Accurate
♥	_____	Talkative

Total   10

What Else Do the Numbers Mean?

For any particular style, if you scored:

8–10 (high) you have a strong tendency to always communicate in this style.

3–7 (middle) you can easily shift into this conversation style from other styles.

0–2 (low) you rarely communicate in this style and might find it difficult to talk to people who converse in this style.

Understanding and Using Different Conversation Styles

I like to think of conversation like dancing. Each person I talk (or dance) with is a new partner with a different conversation style. One partner may be outgoing while the other is reserved. One may prefer heated political discussions while the other enjoys comparing movie reviews. You can use the letters in *C-H-A-T* to help you remember how to adjust your conversation style so you can "dance" with everyone you meet.

> ## Each Letter in the Word *C-H-A-T*
> ## Stands for One of Four Chatting Styles
>
> ### C = Candid
> ### H = Humble
> ### A = Accurate
> ### T = Talkative

C Stands for Candid ♣

If most of your answers fell into the "Candid" category, you have a straightforward approach to conversation.

Your Conversational Strengths

You usually say what's on your mind without mincing words. You most likely thrive on competition of all kinds and often see conversation as a jousting match in which you have the opportunity to debate, argue, or convince someone of your opinion. You love to "mix it up," conversationally speaking, and are fun and beneficial to chat with if people share your sense of humor, intensity, and competitiveness.

Your Conversational Weaknesses

Because you're keenly competitive, you see conversations as a match that you must "win." As a result, others often describe you as blunt, pushy, or too aggressive. You have a tendency to get impatient with people who have a less energetic or direct style. Your habit of "shooting from the lip" often ignores how your directness affects others. People feel that you are at times domineering, boastful, or tactless.

> ## People with a Candid Chatting Style May Like to Talk About
>
> ♣ sports ♣ crime ♣ business heroes ♣ adventure stories ♣ action movies ♣ politics ♣ entrepreneurial endeavors ♣ money and power ♣ military experiences ♣ working out
>
> ## 🖱 Use Your Favorite Search Engine to Find More Career-Related Conversation Topics
>
> Type something like "careers in sports, business management, politics, or military" into your favorite search engine to learn about employment opportunities for people who have a Candid chatting style. Then use that information to explore career-related topics that these people enjoy chatting about.

If you scored low in this category, follow these dos and don'ts when talking to people with the "Candid" style:

- **Do** show a genuine interest in their business and personal goals. These folks love to talk about themselves and their achievements.
- **Don't** get into any debates with them even if they challenge your opinions. They like arguing, are good at it, and usually win.
- **Do** ask for their opinions and advice. You can learn a lot from these goal-oriented people.
- **Don't** go into overly detailed or complex explanations. They are "big picture" thinkers who get impatient discussing minor details.

- **Do** show a self-effacing sense of humor. They like others who are not afraid of laughing at themselves.
- **Don't** take offense if they heckle you or belittle your accomplishments.
- **Do** remember that teasing and put-downs are their way of testing your level of self-confidence.

H Stands for Humble ◆

If most of your answers fell into the "Humble" category, you have a reserved approach to conversation.

Your Conversational Strengths

Thoughtful is the word that describes your conversation style. You are soft-spoken and calm when you do talk. Since your style is nonthreatening, others will open up to you. As a rule, you are an excellent listener and sympathetic to the feelings of others, especially those of people you have already met. It takes you a little time, but once you get to know a person, you open up and converse easily.

Your Conversational Weaknesses

Your tendency to remain passive creates the impression that you are shy, disinterested, snobbish, or unwilling to communicate. You often get overwhelmed by aggressive or talkative types, and clam up when you feel anxious. Your fear of saying the wrong thing, being boring, or offending others inhibits your spontaneity and

People with a Humble Chatting Style May Like to Talk About

♦ relationships ♦ human interest stories ♦ personal stories ♦ movie stars ♦ food ♦ cooking and restaurants ♦ home decorating ♦ art ♦ music ♦ theater ♦ poetry ♦ dance ♦ books ♦ social issues ♦ hobbies ♦ gardening ♦ animals ♦ family

🖱 Use Your Favorite Search Engine to Find More Career-Related Conversation Topics

Type something like "careers in social service, human resources, or fine arts" into your favorite search engine to learn about jobs and employment opportunities for people who have a Humble chatting style. Then use that information to explore career-related topics that these people enjoy chatting about.

often makes the first few minutes of your conversations awkward. If you scored low in this category, follow these dos and don'ts when talking to people with a "Humble" style:

- **Do** show a desire to talk about their interests. These folks need a little extra encouragement to open up.
- **Don't** get aggressive, critical, or argumentative. They turn off almost immediately at the first sign of conflict.
- **Do** ask for their views, feelings, and insights about issues that concern people. They will open up if you let them know you value what they have to say.
- **Don't** interrupt them or complete their sentences. These people often pause to consider their words, so give them

time to finish speaking.

- **Do** encourage them to talk by emphasizing common views and interests. Your interested response is essential for them to reveal their opinions.
- **Don't** give up if the conversation takes a little more time to get going.
- **Do** remember that people with this style take their time before opening up to strangers.

A Stands for Accurate ♠

If most of your answers fell into the "Accurate" category, you have a methodical approach to conversation.

Your Conversational Strengths

Your ability to absorb, assess, and impart information helps you converse about technical topics such as computers, engineering, or other detail- or process-oriented subjects. Your ability to break down procedures from the first detail, then to the next, all the way through to the finish, without skipping any points along the way helps you explain difficult concepts. You enjoy "shop talk" and more serious subjects that require detailed knowledge or problem solving.

Your Conversational Weaknesses

You rarely are the one to "break the ice," so others may see you as shy or unavailable for conversation. Your tendency to go into excruciating detail about specific topics can cause some people to lose interest or become confused about your main point. Your logical approach can give the impression that you have little patience for others who do not understand technical or complicated subjects or think differently than you. You can come across to others

---

People with an Accurate Chatting Style May Like to Talk About

♠ science & math ♠ architecture ♠ computers ♠ design
♠ stock markets ♠ technology ♠ how things work
♠ inventions ♠ science fiction/fantasy ♠ mysteries
♠ home improvement and tools ♠ sports

🖱 Use Your Favorite Search Engine to Find More Career-Related Conversation Topics

Type something like "careers in science, engineering, and technology" into your favorite search engine to learn about jobs and employment opportunities for people who have an Accurate chatting style. Then use that information to explore career-related topics that these people enjoy chatting about.

---

as overly serious because you tend to avoid making "small talk." If you scored low in this category, follow these dos and don'ts when talking to people with an "Accurate" style:

- **Do** praise their technical knowledge. These people like to impress others with their intelligence, so let them.
- **Don't** get into debates or contradict their views. They hate being wrong and take criticism personally.
- **Do** encourage them to talk about subjects outside their specific area of expertise. "Bridge" your conversation to related subjects or look forward to hearing everything you never wanted to know about computer hard drives, pumps, or who knows what else.
- **Don't** change topics too frequently. People with this style prefer to limit the discussion to one topic at a time.

- **Do** gently change the conversation to lighter topics of interest. These folks have a tendency to dwell on serious or tedious topics for too long.
- **Don't** be offended if you hear criticism or offers of unsolicited advice.
- **Do** remember that they see everything as a "problem" to be solved and they want to have all the answers.

T Stands for Talkative ♥

If most of your answers fell into the "Talkative" category, you have an outgoing approach to conversation.

Your Conversational Strengths

You're an extroverted, energetic conversationalist who can talk about anything as long as you have an audience. You thoroughly enjoy interacting with others and being the center of attention. You're perfectly happy to initiate conversations with just about anyone. People see you as a fun and friendly person who is open to contact.

Your Conversational Weaknesses

You can talk too much. Less talkative styles sometimes feel overwhelmed when they talk with you because you come across to these people as overbearing. Your tendency to dominate the conversation and be the center of attention makes others feel left out. You sometimes fail to listen or give others a chance to participate.

People with a Talkative Chatting Style May Like to Talk About

♥ themselves ♥ friends and family ♥ travel ♥ food and entertainment ♥ pop culture ♥ hobbies ♥ self-improvement ♥ successful people ♥ unusual media stories ♥ humorous events ♥ hopes and dreams ♥ pets ♥ any topic that isn't technical or complicated

🖱 Use Your Favorite Search Engine to Find More Career-Related Conversation Topics

Type something like "careers for talkative people" into your favorite search engine to learn about jobs and employment opportunities for people who like to talk. Then use that information to explore career-related topics that these people enjoy chatting about.

If you scored low in this category, follow these dos and don'ts when talking to people with a "Talkative" style:

- **Do** let them have center stage. They crave recognition and attention, so show you appreciate their efforts.
- **Don't** get into detailed explanations about technical topics or difficult concepts. They'll just get confused, frustrated, and bored.
- **Do** share your interests with them. If you don't, they'll talk your ear off.
- **Don't** feel bad when you interrupt them to speak. If you don't speak up, you will never get a word in edgewise.

- **Do** be playful, show your sense of humor, and—above all—laugh at their jokes. They really want others to like them and think that they are funny.
- **Don't** discuss heavy topics or get too serious.
- **Do** remember that having fun in a conversation is one of their top priorities.

Blend the Four Styles to Be a Well-Rounded Conversationalist

While most people seem to lean toward one conversation style, they probably have a few strengths and weaknesses from each of the four styles. Here are four ways to help blend your style with the other three styles and improve your conversations with practically everyone you talk to:

- Recognize your strengths and weaknesses in each of the styles.
- Build on your strengths and eliminate your weaknesses from each style.
- Adjust your conversational style to "dance" with the styles of others.
- Practice chatting with people whose style is different from your own.

FAQ
How do you immediately recognize the conversation style of a stranger?

You'll soon recognize the conversation style of strangers when you pay close attention to body language and how the first few minutes of the conversation progress. Is she outgoing or shy? Does he like to make small talk or only "shop talk"? Is she direct and to the point or reserved? Is he argumentative or easygoing?

Make it a habit to observe the four styles as you talk to the people around you at work, home, the store—everywhere! In no time, your success will soar when talking to new and old acquaintances. Plus, you'll have a lot more fun on those "spins" around the conversational dance floor.

17

Talking to People from Other Countries

Guides cannot master the subtleties of the American joke.
—Mark Twain, a.k.a. Samuel Clemens (1835–1910), writer, humorist

Do you know how to talk and act with people from other countries without offending them, being offended, or putting yourself into embarrassing situations? Since friendliness and good intentions may not always bridge the gap that exists between cultures, remember these dos and dont's when speaking to people whose backgrounds and cultures differ from your own.

- **Do** respect differences.
- **Don't** be shy about introducing yourself.
- **Do** show interest in the other person's country.
- **Don't** take offense if someone says the wrong thing.
- **Do** avoid stereotyping.
- **Don't** assume you know the country a person is from.
- **Do** match your speaking speed and vocabulary with the person's language skills.
- **Don't** assume understanding.
- **Do** talk about upbeat topics.
- **Don't** talk about depressing topics.

Do Respect Differences

Many countries around the world have become "melting pots" of cultures, and today's society has more diverse traditions, religions, and ethnic groups than ever before. By assuming that people from other countries share your values, attitudes, and ways of communicating, you can fall into social blunders or uncomfortable conversations. However, if you remember that people from different countries frequently have different styles of talking and acting, then you'll be less likely to be offended or give offense.

FAQ

Is it true that Americans are more informal than people from other countries?

Although Americans are known for their friendliness, their informality isn't always appreciated or understood by people from other countries. "Coming on too strong, too soon" is a common complaint heard about Americans by those who prefer a more formal manner with people they don't know well. In general, use a more reserved conversation style when you meet people from countries other than the United States.

Don't Be Shy about Introducing Yourself

"Hello, my name is Don Gabor" is a perfectly acceptable way to start conversations with foreigners in most social and business situations. This friendly and typically American greeting shows others that you want to talk to them. While etiquette experts still frown upon using someone's first name before being given permission, most Americans seem to do it anyway. However, many British, Europeans, Middle Easterners, and Asians prefer to use their titles (Mr., Mrs., Miss, or Dr.) and last names when they talk to new acquaintances. Although the custom of shaking hands when meeting a stranger is a generally accepted practice in most countries, there are many exceptions. The chart in the next chapter shows you customary ways to greet people from various countries around the world.

Tip on Remembering Foreign or Uncommon Names

When a name is unfamiliar or difficult to pronounce, ask the person to spell it for you and to say it correctly. Picture what the letters spell phonetically or sound similar to. For example, if you meet Vanya Roussetzki, think: Vawn-ya Rose-ETZ-skee. It may take you several times to get it right, but most foreigners feel flattered when you use and remember their names.

After chatting for a while, you may feel like the time is right to move to a first-name basis. Then you can say, "Please call me (your first name)." Depending on the other person's preference and the situation, he may follow your lead. If not, continue to use his title and last name until you are invited to do otherwise.

Do Show Interest in the Other Person's Country

Show genuine curiosity and interest in the other person's country by seeking general background information about his or her homeland. The more appreciation you show for her culture, the greater the likelihood she will open up and talk to you. As you talk, listen and observe carefully for topics and behaviors to expand upon and those to avoid. Find out all you can about her country, town, people, food, music, and so on, and you will have plenty of conversational fuel. Always take care to steer clear of conversations about sex, politics, and religion. These traditionally "taboo topics" are highly charged and can lead to disagreements.

However, you can feel free to ask more ritual, information-seeking questions such as: "Tell me a little about the town where you are from," or "What's it like where you grew up (used to live, etc.)?" or "What kinds of work do people do where you live?" or "Is your town or area known for any special tourist attractions?" or "What kinds of things do people in your town do for fun?"

While many people from foreign countries like to practice their English, they are usually delighted if you ask them to teach you a few ritual phrases in their native language. This technique is a great way to build rapport and show appreciation for their country and culture. For example, you can ask, "How do you say 'Hello,' 'Good-bye,' 'Please,' 'Thank you,' and 'How are you?' in Greek (Japanese, Polish, etc.)?" Then, when you see the person the next time, say a few words in his language and watch his smile and eyes light up!

Don't Take Offense if Someone Says the Wrong Thing

What should you say if a foreigner makes a sweeping generalization about your country or the place where you live, and you don't agree? First, don't take offense or start to argue. Instead, you can say something like "It might appear that way to you, but I don't think most people who live here share that view, myself included."

With the many regional differences that exist in most countries, it comes as no surprise that newcomers may not be tuned in to local customs or etiquette. Questions that you might consider personal, such as "How much did you pay?" or "Why don't you have any children?" might be perfectly acceptable in the other person's homeland.

Rather than be offended by personal questions, view them as a genuine curiosity about your lifestyle and culture. You can offer a general response, such as "People in my profession earn anywhere between . . . and . . . a year, depending on their education and experience," or "There are lots of married couples in this country who don't have children, and I'm sure that they all have their own reasons." If the person presses the point, and you don't want to be more specific, say, "Most people here consider questions like that personal, so I'd rather not say," or "That's a topic that I don't feel comfortable discussing."

Do Avoid Stereotyping

Although people from particular countries or regions around the world often share similar customs and conversational styles, resist the urge to lump everyone together with generalized statements. Never stereotype people with comments such as "You French (Germans, Chinese, Indians, or whoever) always . . ." Better conversations develop with people from other countries when you ask them for their individual opinions, views, and feelings.

Don't Assume You Know the Country a Person Is From

"You're not from England? But you sound so English!" This conversational blunder happens a lot to people who speak with what sounds like a British accent. In fact, they may be from South Africa, New Zealand, Australia, Ireland, Scotland, Wales, India, Canada, Ghana, Belize, Hong Kong, Zimbabwe, or any other of the fifty independent nations or protectorates that were once British colonies.

People are usually offended if you make incorrect assumptions about their nationality based on their appearance, language, or accent. For example, French—the mother tongue of more than 90 million people around the globe—is spoken in Quebec, Haiti, Guinea, Indochina, Morocco, Algeria, and several other countries in the Caribbean and North Africa. Spanish is the most widely spoken Romance language in the world. It is the official language of Spain and most of Latin America, with more than 14.5 million Spanish-speaking people in the United States, many of whom are

American-born. Assuming that a person is from Mexico, for example, because she speaks Spanish could be embarrassing.

English-speaking Canadians dislike being taken for Americans, although it happens all the time. French Canadians will fiercely correct anyone who suggests that they are from France. Asians of one nationality are greatly offended if they are confused with Asians of another nationality. You could start a small war if you confuse a Greek and a Turk, or an Israeli with a Palestinian. Like other examples of cultural faux pas, the list goes on and on.

Avoid assumptions about people's origins by carefully listening for any geographical references that might provide clues to where their homeland is. If you hear a particular city name, for example, you can ask, "You went to school in Hong Kong? Is that where you are from?" If you're not sure, avoid the tendency to guess. It is okay to be direct and ask, "Where are you from?" or "Where did you grow up?" or "Where were you born?"

Do Match Your Speaking Speed and Vocabulary with the Person's Language Skills

Let's face it, learning a new language is tough, especially with all the slang, idioms, abbreviations, and jargon that fill daily conversations. When you first meet someone whose native language is not your own, speak slowly and keep your sentences short until you can determine his or her level of understanding. If there is a language barrier, be patient and follow one international host's excellent advice: "Keep it simple, don't talk loudly, and never act like you are speaking to a child."

Be aware that many people feel self-conscious about their ability to speak a foreign language and may need a little extra encouragement from you to carry on a conversation. If the person suggests that his or her language skills are inadequate, you can say, "I think you speak quite well! How long have you been studying the language?"

Using a Smartphone to Instantly Find More Country-Specific Topics of Conversation

Do you attend business or social events where there are guests from other countries, but you may not know much about where they are from? The solution may be at your fingertips if you have a "smartphone" and access to the Internet. Log onto your favorite search engine's website and type in the name of the person's home country. You'll see scores of links to tourist organizations, travel guides, country fact books, history and geography websites—all packed with information that you can quickly access and use to break the ice and engage foreign guests in conversations about their own country.

Don't Assume Understanding

Over the course of your conversation, be sure to check that the other person understands you. Even when they don't fully comprehend your meaning or intent, people with limited foreign language skills often nod their heads or say "Yes" if you ask, "Do you understand?"

You can avoid many misunderstandings by asking questions that require the other person to restate or paraphrase what you have said. For example, you can say, "Just to make sure you understand how to find our house, why don't you repeat the directions to me." Or you can restate what you think he or she has said. For example, "I just want to make sure that I understand you correctly. You want me to . . . Is that right?"

If you find that your message did not get through, then try restating it more directly and in fewer words. You can say, "Let me say it a different way."

FAQ

I know to avoid discussing sex, politics, and religion, but what topics are okay to bring up when I'm talking with someone from another country?

Do Talk about Upbeat Topics

Most people from other countries enjoy exchanging views on a variety of subjects that reveal their interests, experiences, and tastes. For example, you can talk about:

American culture	entrepreneurs	outdoor activities
animals	family life*	professions
art	fashion	scenery/geography
business/work	food and drink	science/technology
cars	gardening	sports
city/country life	history*	tourist attractions
culture/heritage	hobbies	travel
current events*	language	volunteer work
customs	literature	weather/climate
entertainment	music	world affairs*

*Caution: Take care when discussing these topics, as they can lead to strong differences of opinion or uncomfortable conversations. Here are a few examples of how to start a conversation using some of these topics:

What are the surroundings like where you live back home? (scenery/geography)
What is your city or town like? (city/country life)
What do you find most interesting about life here? (American culture)
When you have time off from work, what do you like to do? (hobbies)

Tell me a little about your town's history. (culture/heritage)
How do you compare doing business here with doing it at home in your country? (business/work)
Have you recently seen any movies (plays, music, etc.) that you liked? (entertainment)
If I were to visit your country (city, etc.), where would you suggest that I go? (travel)
Who do you think is likely to win the World Cup (soccer) this year? (sports)

Don't Talk about Depressing Topics

Avoid discussing the following topics with people from other countries until you know them better. These controversial topics can polarize people and put them into a somber mood, particularly in social or business situations:

alcohol/drug abuse	ethnic humor	radical unrest
apartheid	internal politics	regional conflicts
brutal crimes	money problems	religion
Cold War	organized crime	sex
colonialism	personal illness	taxes
communism	politics	terrorism
economic problems	poverty	tragedies

FAQ

How do you sustain a friendship with someone from a different country?

Once you've met someone from another country, the next step is to build the friendship, and the key is to maintain contact. Send your new friend a letter, postcard, or e-mail to say how much you enjoyed meeting him and that you'd like to become Facebook friends. Remembering his birthday or a special event will help cement the relationship. E-mail has made it possible to have nearly instant contact with people all over the world, so it's now easier than ever to be in contact. With some international long-distance telephone calling plans, you can talk to people thousands of miles away for reasonable rates. Of course, try to meet your friend in person whenever it's possible.

Conversing with People from Other Countries Builds Bridges of Friendship

Someone long ago once said that the world is like a book, and those who do not travel read only one page. Today, however, with so many people from around the world traveling or living abroad, you have the opportunity to meet foreigners in your hometown.

Discovering new foods, customs, music, business opportunities, perspectives, and values are only a few of the many benefits you have to gain from conversing with people from around the world. But the biggest reward of all when you meet and talk to people who are different from you is that of mutual understanding and international friendship.

18

Customs That Influence Cross-cultural Conversations

The more I traveled, the more I realized that fear makes strangers of people who should be friends.
—Shirley MacLaine (1934–), American actress

"I can't believe she asked me how much my engagement ring cost!" "Okay, so I'm five minutes late. What's the big deal?" "I wish that he wouldn't stand so close to me when we speak."

Talking to people from other countries can be challenging, especially when you have little knowledge of their cultural sensitivities and taboos. That's why the more you know about a person's culture and homeland, the less likely you will say the wrong thing or be offended by his or her customs.

How Savvy Are You about the Customs of Other Cultures?

Take this True/False quiz and find out how much you know about talking to people from other countries. The answers are at the end of the quiz.

1. Japanese like a strong handshake when they meet strangers.   T __ F __

2. Being only a few minutes late to an appointment will upset a German.   T __ F __

3. North Americans stand closer than Latin Americans when they talk.   T __ F __

4. Chinese gesture with their hands when
   they speak.   T __ F __

5. Using first names is customary in the U.S.
   but considered rude by Europeans, Asians,
   and Latin Americans if done so without
   permission.   T __ F __

6. All cultures view lack of eye contact as a
   sign of dishonesty.   T __ F __

7. Women should offer to shake hands with
   men from the Middle East.   T __ F __

8. Bulgarians and Greeks nod their heads when
   they disagree.   T __ F __

9. South Americans consider it rude to back
   away in a conversation.   T __ F __

10. Italians never make small talk before
    bringing up business issues.   T __ F __

11. A woman from India would be offended
    if you pointed at her with your finger.   T __ F __

12. Africans enjoy talking about music, art,
    sculpture, and oral literature.   T __ F __

13. Filipinos rarely say no to or argue with
    foreigners.   T __ F __

14. Casual and informal conversations are
    typical of most people from the Caribbean.   T __ F __

15. The topic of soccer would bore most
    Central Americans.   T __ F __

Answers

1. False: Although Japanese are accustomed to shaking
   hands with Westerners, they prefer a light handshake.

2. True: Punctuality is of the upmost importance to Germans. They consider it rude when someone is even a few minutes late to a business or social engagement.

3. False: North Americans prefer to stand about three feet from the people they speak with. Latin Americans speak at a distance of one to two feet.

4. False: Chinese rarely speak with their hands and find it distracting when speaking with people who do.

5. True: Americans love to use first names from the moment they are introduced, although many foreigners consider it to be too informal.

6. False: Mexicans, for example, often avert their eyes out of respect.

7. False: Strict religious rules prohibit Muslims and Orthodox Jews from having physical contact with the opposite sex in public.

8. True: Bulgarians and Greeks shake their heads from side to side when they mean yes and nod their heads when they mean no.

9. True: Backing away during a conversation is considered rude by South Americans because they like to stand very close while they chat.

10. False: Be prepared to make conversation about your family, travel, food, and so on before discussing any business matters with Italians.

11. True: People from India consider it rude to point with a finger. They point with their chins.

12. True: Africans like to discuss the influence of their traditional music, art, sculpture, and oral literature on jazz, blues, modern art, and modern dance.

13. True: Filipinos value harmony in conversations and consider the word *no* impolite.

14. True: People from the Caribbean usually have a more relaxed style of talking than do Americans, British, French, Spanish, or Dutch.

15. False: Central Americans are passionate about soccer, as are most Europeans, Mexicans, and South Americans.

How Do Your Skills Rate?

Number of correct answers	Level/follow-up
13–15	Super! You know how to talk to just about anyone from anywhere. Dig even deeper to find out more about the many subcultures that exist within each country and culture.
9–12	Pretty good! You are aware of many foreign customs that influence conversation. Zero in on the many exceptions that exist within cultures, so you don't assume too much when talking to someone from a particular country.
5–8	Okay, but . . . You know enough about people from other countries to have a conversation, but you might find yourself saying something embarrassing or offensive. Ask them more questions about where they are from and some of their customs. Continue your conversation based on the information they tell you.
0–4	Oops! You are at risk of saying the wrong thing when you talk to people from other countries. Learn more about the cultures and customs of

other countries so that when you converse, you won't put your foot in your mouth. If you ask questions, show interest, listen carefully, and observe their behavior, you'll quickly improve.

Use the Following Chart to Avoid Embarrassing Situations and Taboo Topics

It is easy to misinterpret actions of acquaintances and friends from other countries if you are unaware of their particular communication styles, customs, and taboos. The following chart summarizes greetings, conversation styles, body language, plus certain actions and topics to avoid while socializing with people from various countries and regions of the world. These traits are generalizations and the list does not include all nationalities, but the information is representative of the people whom you will most likely encounter at home, at work, and in business or social situations.

FAQ

Will making generalizations about the foreigners I meet make them feel like I don't see them as individuals?

It is always important not to stereotype the people you meet. Be aware that you are speaking with individuals and that there are many cultural variations within countries and regions. To avoid saying or doing the wrong thing, observe, listen, and follow the other person's lead as you meet and converse. And remember to always be polite, mind your manners, and *never* say, "But I thought everyone from your country . . ."

Conversation Customs Chart

Country/Region	Handshake/Greeting	Conversation Style
Central Africa*	medium	polite/leisurely
North Africa*	medium (men only)	unhurried
South Africa*	medium	polite/formal
Brazil	medium	outgoing
Canada	medium	relaxed/polite
Caribbean*	medium	informal
Central America*	light	polite/formal
China*	light/bow	reserved
Eastern Europe*	firm	outgoing
England	light	formal
France	light	proud/formal
Germany	firm	practical/formal
Greece	light	laid-back
India*	medium (men only)	leisurely
Israel	medium (men only)	to the point
Italy	light	demonstrative
Japan	light	reserved
Mexico	medium	friendly
Middle East*	medium (men only)	unhurried
Philippines	firm	social/formal
Poland	medium	demonstrative
Russia*	medium	demonstrative
Scandinavia	firm	reserved/formal
South America*	light-medium	personal
Southeast Asia*	light/nod	reserved
United States	firm	friendly/informal

*   These countries and regions are ethnically diverse with a wide variety of cultures and customs.

Eye Contact	Standing Distance	Taboo Actions/Topics
medium	2–3 ft.	religion/political conflicts
medium	1–2 ft.	Middle East politics
medium	2–3 ft.	apartheid
strong	1–2 ft.	backing away
medium	3 ft.	mistaken for American
medium	2 ft.	drug trade
strong	1–2 ft.	backing away
light	3–4 ft.	mistaken for Japanese
medium	2–3 ft.	Communist rule
light	3 ft.	standing too close
strong	1–2 ft.	criticizing
medium	2–3 ft.	World War II
medium	2–3 ft.	refusing food
medium	2–3 ft.	saying *no*
medium	1–2 ft.	World War II
medium	1–2 ft.	organized crime
light	3–4 ft.	mistaken for Chinese
medium-light	1–2 ft.	backing away
strong	1–2 ft.	eating with left hand
light	2–3 ft.	hands on hips
medium	2–3 ft.	World War II
medium	1–2 ft.	criticizing
strong	2–3 ft.	loud outbursts
strong	1–2 ft.	backing away
limited	3–4 ft.	confrontation
medium	2–3 ft.	criticizing

More Ways to Learn about the Customs of People from Other Countries

In addition to talking to people about their homelands, you can take advantage of the many opportunities where you live to learn about other countries and cultures.

Visit or Attend

- restaurants that serve food from other countries or cultures
- cultural events that feature music, dance, art, and food*
- cultural centers related to a particular country or culture
- foreign language classes*
- international centers
- volunteer programs to tutor people who want to learn your language
- lectures or classes about a country's customs or culture*
- museums that feature art from other countries
- folk dance classes or music classes*
- libraries where you can research places that you've always wanted to visit.

Read about Other Countries in

- *National Geographic* magazine
- travel and food sections of newspapers and magazines
- travel guides such as *Fodor's, Frommer's, Insight, Michelin,* and *The Rough Guides*
- newspaper features or human interest stories
- nonfiction or photography books
- novels that are set in and have characters from other countries.

---

* Of course, in addition to learning more about a particular country or culture, many of these places provide a great opportunity to meet people and make new friends!

Watch Movies or Television Programs from Other Countries That

- show how people there live
- present history and cultural development
- reveal historical perspectives about the people who live there
- discuss popular sporting events.

Websites Offer the Fastest Way to Learn More about International Customs

The Internet offers an endless supply of websites, books, and blogs about the customs of most countries. Understanding and using foreign customs is particularly important when you travel for business abroad or entertain foreign clients in the United States, and it's easy to find that information. Simply type "customs in other countries" into your favorite search engine and you'll see dozens of links to useful references.

Respectful Conversations Yield International Friendships

Adding new knowledge, respect, and tolerance for individual differences is the key to communicating effectively with foreigners. Every social and business situation holds the potential for rewarding conversations that allow the people from varying cultures to talk and learn about each other. As you become more comfortable with different communication styles, body language, customs, and taboos, many of your conversations will lead you to new friends from around the world.

19

60 Ways to Improve Your Conversations and Build Lasting Friendships

> Let the world know you as you are, not as you think you should be—because sooner or later, if you are posing, you will forget the pose and then where are you?
> —Fanny Brice (1891–1951), singer and comedian

Here are some final tips to keep in mind when starting, continuing, and ending conversations.

Starting Conversations

1. Be the first to say hello and greet people you see regularly.
2. Look for people who display open body language.
3. Smile and use eye contact when you meet people.
4. Introduce or reintroduce yourself to others.
5. Break the ice with confidence: Don't anticipate rejection.
6. Go out of your way to meet new people.
7. Show curiosity and interest in others.
8. Seek common interests, goals, and experiences when you meet people.
9. Make an effort to help people if you can.
10. Take time to be cordial with your neighbors and coworkers.
11. Be open to making small talk and answering common ritual questions.

12. Compliment others about what they are wearing, doing, or saying.
13. Encourage others to talk with you by smiling and making eye contact with them.
14. Ask a person's name if you have forgotten it.
15. Use the person's name when you are reconnecting.
16. Join other conversations already in progress.
17. Be ready to briefly tell others what you do for a living and for fun.
18. Ask questions about what others do for a living and for fun.
19. Know what to say next by listening between the lines for key words, implied messages, and possible conversation topics.
20. Show others that you are a good listener by restating their comments and asking related follow-up questions.

Continuing Conversations

21. Communicate enthusiasm and optimism through your conversations and sense of humor.
22. Don't complain or talk about negative topics or gory news stories.
23. When you tell a story or relate an experience, present the main point first, then add the supporting details.
24. Tell other people about the important events in your life.
25. Find out about the big things in the lives of others.
26. Be receptive to new ideas.
27. Look for the positive in those you meet.
28. Ask others about things they have told you in previous conversations.
29. Keep your exchanges balanced: Don't talk too much or too little.
30. Always search for another person's "hot buttons" or high-interest topics.

31. Use the person's name periodically in conversation.
32. Laugh when others say something amusing.
33. Tell others something interesting or challenging about what you do.
34. Let others play the expert.
35. Keep abreast of current events and the issues that affect all of our lives.
36. Express your feelings, opinions, and emotions to others.
37. Ask other people their opinions to show you value their perspective.
38. Accept a person's right to think and feel differently about things than you do.
39. Change topics before discussions get emotional or overheated.
40. Change the topic of conversation by saying, "I heard you mention earlier . . ."
41. Explore a variety of topics to see which ones have more for you to talk about.
42. Show interest in others by asking open-ended questions.
43. Balance disclosing and receiving background and personal information.
44. Speak about a variety of topics and subjects, including but not limited to your work.
45. Use open body language to show others that you are enjoying your conversations.

Ending Conversations and Building Friendships That Last

46. Identify one or two common interests before ending the conversation.
47. Close your conversation on a positive topic.
48. Send a "closing signal" before ending the exchange by saying, "I've enjoyed chatting with you."
49. Before concluding your conversation, ask, "What's the best way to stay in touch with you?"

50. End your conversation with the person's name, a warm handshake, and a smile.
51. Follow up soon after you've met to reinforce the contact.
52. Keep in touch with friends and acquaintances via telephone, e-mail, Facebook, LinkedIn, Twitter, or other social networks.
53. Invite new friends to join you for dinner, social events, or other activities where you can get to know one another better.
54. Let your friendship develop at a natural pace.
55. Balance offering and accepting social invitations.
56. Introduce new friends to your old friends.
57. Accept your friends as they are: Don't try to change them.
58. Never violate your friends' trust or confidence.
59. Make seeing your friends on a regular basis a lifestyle choice.
60. Maintain and nurture your friendships and they can last a lifetime.

Conclusion

Here you have all the tips and communication skills you need to begin and sustain conversations. Now it's up to you to get out there and meet people. You'll find that with practice, patience, and a positive attitude, you have nothing to lose and a lot to gain. Taking part in stimulating and rewarding conversations will become a reality. All you have to do is look somebody in the eye, smile, and start a conversation!

Index

restaurants *(cont.)*
first dates and, 149–50
Meetup groups and, 116, 118
see also dinners
rhymes, 56
risk, 80
breaking the ice and, 17, 32–33
self-disclosure and, 46–47
ritual questions, 38, 176
breaking the ice with, 18–27,
33–34, 192
hot buttons and, 65–66
self-disclosure and, 42–43
in sustaining conversations, 63,
65–66, 72
romances, romance, 80, 98, 146

sarcasm, 110–11
self-disclosure, 41–49, 69, 105, 141
of employment, 42–44
of feelings and personal experiences,
46–47
in first dates, 147, 151–53, 156, 158
hints about, 47–48
of hopes, dreams, loves, joys, and
sorrows, 45–47
hot buttons and, 42, 64–67
levels of, 43–47, 49
of overly personal information, 48–49
prudence for, 41–43, 47–48
in small amounts over time, 47–48
sustaining conversations and, 69, 194
on your own terms, 41–42
sensitivity, 46–7, 67, 73, 150, 183
sex, 113, 118, 153
foreigners and, 175, 180–81
Shevlin, Mark, 148
short meetings, 131
shyness:
breaking the ice and, 17, 33
conversation styles and, 165, 167, 171
in first dates, 145–46, 150
with foreigners, 173–75
silences, 81, 85, 143, 155
Simonson, Itamar, 145
sincerity, 26–28, 131

singles, xiv–xv, 32
see also dating websites; first dates
small talk, 135, 146, 184, 192
at business events, 70–71
conversation styles and, 161, 168, 172
in sustaining conversations, 68–74
topics and, 69–72
smiles, smiling, 52, 103, 135, 176, 196
body language and, 3–5, 9–11, 13–14
breaking the ice and, 23–24, 28–29,
31–32, 192–93
ending conversations and, 9–10,
87–89, 195
eye contact and, 11–12
first dates and, 150, 154–55
in photos, 106–7
social distance, 8
social events, 195
foreigners and, 179, 185, 191
friends and, xv, 133, 135, 143
networking and, 123, 125
see also dinners; parties
social networks, 93–114, 116, 143, 182,
195
blogs on, 98–100
conversation channels and, xiii–xiv
getting started with, 94–95
joining of, 93–95, 101, 111
Meetup groups and, 115–19
niche, 98–99
online conversations and, 94–96, 98,
103, 108–14
online dating, xvi, 94, 97–98, 102–3,
105
online profiles for, 94–98, 101–7, 112
for professional contacts, 95–96, 99
searching online for, 98–99
softening techniques, 3–13, 16
standing distance, 8, 23
of foreigners, 183, 185, 189
staring, 11, 13
starting conversations, xi, 130, 146
making friends and, 134–35
ways for, 18
see also breaking the ice
stereotyping, 42, 173, 177, 183–84, 187

Don Gabor
Author, Communication Trainer, and "Small Talk" Expert

Don Gabor shows people how to use conversation to connect with others at home, work, and everywhere in between. He trains professionals from all disciplines how to grow their revenues by starting profitable conversations and teaches executives, managers, and staff how to enhance customer service and work together more effectively.

Don is the author of ten books and audio programs on interpersonal communication skills and has been writing books, offering communication programs, and consulting since 1980. He has presented workshops to Professional Association of SQL Servers, Marriott Hotels, Korin Japanese Trading Corp., and many other large and small companies, professional associations, and colleges.

For individuals who want personalized training, Don also offers one-on-one coaching for speeches, presentations, conversation skills, and media training. Don was a media spokesperson for Grand Marnier, Sprint, and Frito-Lay.

As a frequent media guest, his books have been featured in hundreds of print, radio, and television interviews, including *60 Minutes with Andy Rooney*, *Good Day NY*, *Entrepreneur*, the *New York Times*, *Investor's Business Daily*, *Bottom Line*, and many others. The *New Yorker* called Don "a gifted conversationalist." He has been a member of the National Speakers Association since 1991 and served as the president of the New York City chapter (2010–2011).

For information about Don Gabor's programs and how he can help you achieve your communication goals or speak to your organization, contact him at (718) 768-0824 or Don@DonGabor.com or visit his website at www.DonGabor.com.